ALEXANDER RISEMAN

To Hell and Back

First published by Independently Published 1994

First edition

ISBN: 9798507940431

*This book was professionally typeset on Reedsy.
Find out more at reedsy.com*

.

Contents

Foreword

I loved my grandfather not because he was a war hero, or a Holocaust Survivor or just a fabulous grandfather; I loved him because when he was ill at the end of his life, and I asked him how he was, he responded with a twinkle in his eye 'Mustn't Grumble'. He lived a life so few of us are able to; a life of not having all the answers, not understanding why or how, but yet embracing and moving forward and weaving all his experiences into the tapestry called his life.

I think what always strikes me about any Holocaust story, and especially my grandfather's, is that his story could have happened to anyone. And that is why his story of hope, courage and survival is so important to share with the world.

He taught me to keep going even when I was ready to give up life. He taught me that there are good people in the world as well as bad people. He taught me that we can laugh and smile and cry and all that is ok. He believed in family and friendship first and foremost.

He would not want us to hype up his character, although he deserves pages of accolades explaining why he was such an incredible person; he was a devoted husband, father, grandfather and great-grandfather. He also recognised that there is intergenerational trauma passed on because both him and his wife didn't have a regular childhood and I'm sure this would have impacted the childhood they gave their children including my mother.

He was self aware and the most inspirational role model because he was a regular person making the most of his life. He lost his relationship with G-d, he found G-d. He experienced incredible life moments and also dreadful unspeakable suffering. He saw the worst in people and he saw the best. He knew himself and he knew his strengths and weaknesses.

He was himself and we loved him for it. He taught me that it's ok not to be perfect, it is ok to have flaws. He taught me that sometimes life will bring you to your knees in pain and knock all the breath out of you. And that the same life can bring the greatest happiness one could dream of.

Sharon Schurder
  May 2021

Alexander and Sharon in 2010

Introduction

I t is barely 50 years since these atrocities took place, and already some people are denying that they ever happened. I feel it is my duty while I am still alive to record the truth of my own experiences for future generations.

I would also like to leave a memorial for my children and grandchildren, and also for those who want to know the true story of the Jews and the tragic events that took place in the Second World War.

I thank the Lord who has given me the health and strength to do this, as millions of Jews perished and their voices are stilled forever.

This book is dedicated to their memory and to the memory of my dear parents.

THE BRITISH LIBRARY

NATIONAL SOUND ARCHIVE
THE NATIONAL LIFE STORY COLLECTION

NATIONAL LIFE STORY

AWARDS

1994

TO: ALEXANDER RISEMAN

This is to certify that your entry has been accepted
for the first National Life Story Awards
and will thereby be added to the British Library's Collections

Sir Anthony Kenny

CHAIRMAN
BRITISH LIBRARY BOARD

Lord Briggs

CHAIRMAN
NATIONAL LIFE STORY COLLECTION

Professor Paul Thompson

DIRECTOR
NATIONAL LIFE STORY COLLECTION

JUDGES

Tricia Adams   Joanna Bornat   Lord Briggs   Penelope Lively   Jane Mace
Anne Paul   Rob Perks   Harold Rosen   Dorothy Sheridan   Paul Thompson   Katherine Tousey

Alexander Riseman wrote his life story in 1994 at age 68 for his grandchildren. It was submitted and accepted for the National Life Story Awards and was added to the British Library's Collection.

Pre War

I was born Alexander Rajzman in Lodz in 1926, but for many years I have been known as Alexander Riseman. My parents called me Sender. I lived in Lodz with my parents Pinchas and Leah, my sister Rachel who was two years older than me, and my brother Yitzchok who is 19 months younger than me. My mother's maiden name was Engel.

We kept in close touch with all our uncles, aunts, cousins, nephews and nieces. I remember that we were a large and very happy extended family. I only have happy memories of my childhood until the war broke out.

Before the First World War Lodz was occupied by Russia. It was in the centre of Poland and was an industrial city famous for its textiles. It was known as the Manchester of Europe and was the second largest Jewish community in Europe (Warsaw was the largest).

The entire population of Lodz before the War was approximately 800,000 people. A third were Jews, a third were ethnic Germans and the remainder were Poles.

Before the 1939 war the Jews and the Germans in Lodz lived in harmony. They got on with the Germans better than with the Poles. One of the reasons was because they were both connected with the production of textiles. The Germans were mostly employed as weaves; while the Jews were mainly the finishers and manufacturers of the finished garments.

Another reason was that spoken Yiddish is very similar to German, so that there was no communication problem. Also, we shared a common bond as the Germans were also a minority group.

We had a German neighbour and I used to play with one of his children. I remember my father holding me on one knee, and the neighbour's child on the other, while he told us stories.

My father's parents came from Kielce, which is a large town in Eastern Poland. I only knew my father's parents because they also lived in Lodz. They came there at the turn of the century because at that time Lodz was becoming an industrial city and so it attracted a lot of Jews from smaller towns.

My mother's father came from Szydlow, which is a small town in Eastern Poland. He was the schochet of that town. To be a schochet one had to be a learned man and to have studied Talmud for many years. He was called Sender the Schochet and I was named after him. Next to the Rabbi a schochet was the most prominent person in the community. He and his wife died before I was born.

Both my mother and my father came from very large families.

All my mother's brothers were Talmudei Chachomim (learned laymen). They were much older than my mother as she was the youngest in the family.

Three of her brothers lived in Lodz, their names were Shmiel, Usher and Hirsch Leib, who was the oldest. The fourth one was called Benjomin who lived in a little town called Opatow (Apt), which is in Eastern Poland. Her fifth brother Fischel lived in Berlin.

My uncle Shmiel used to come into us nearly every day, and my mother always gave him a meal. He was a very clever man and a great Talmud Chochom. Everyone in the family used to go to him for advice.

He had two sons and two daughters. The oldest son was called Chaim who married before the war. The younger son was called Sender, who is still alive today and lives in Israel. The daughters were called Sara and Chaya. They also live in Israel.

My uncle Shmiel and his wife Bloomah lived in one room, together with their four children. The room also provided their living, as it contained the knitting machines. It was normal for people to live and work in the same room.

My uncle Usher used to deliver the milk. He carried two milk churns, one on his chest and one on his back, connected with a leather shoulder belt. Whenever he came to us he rested, and my mother always made him something to eat.

My father (middle), mother (2nd from left), brother Yitzchok (2nd from right), sister Rachel (left) and myself (right)

My uncle Benjomin used to sit and study all day, while his wife Nacha looked after the business. They owned a large general store in the market, where they sold everything needed for the household, from pots and pans to crockery, bed linen, textiles and clothing.

Nacha used to come to Lodz from time to time to buy new stock for their store. When she made these business trips she used to stay with us. In those days it was normal for relatives to come and stay with other relations.

My uncle Fischel lived in Berlin until 1933 when Hitler came to power. He went to live in France where he became a schochet and Kashrus supervisor on a large French liner that had many Jewish passengers.

His family managed to emigrate to Palestine before the war broke out. When war broke out and France was occupied by the Germans the Vichy government in France arrested him. They were going to deport him to a concentration camp in Eastern Europe, but somehow, he escaped and he managed to join his family in Palestine.

Later on, one of his sons became a General in the Israeli army, and he changed his name from Engle to Gan El.

My mother had one sister called Malka, who lived with her husband, called Yisroel, in Lodz. They had two sons. They lived in the poorer part of town in a three-storey house built completely of timber. On the ground floor there were weaving machines.

My aunt Malka lived in one room on the second floor of this building. Every time we visited her my mother took with her a chicken and some meat and fish together with some money for Shabbos, as they were very poor.

My uncle Yisroel was always out of work. He was very handy and he made lots of toys for his two boys. Whenever we visited them he used to take us all to the park which was near his house and play games with us, so we always looked forward to going there.

One of his sons (my cousin) was called Alter who used to draw lots of different things. As I was also good at drawing we had something in common.

My father had four brothers. One died before the war from Tuberculosis. His wife and younger daughter died soon after him, also from TB. This disease was prevalent before the war, and it was usually fatal.

The second brother Calman Coppel, I don't remember very well. The third brother Hirsch Myer and his wife Sheindel were the ones who shared their room with us when we lived in the Ghetto, until they were deported.

Then there was the youngest brother whose name was Avrom Fisher. He was tall and very good looking. There was consternation in the family when he had his call up papers to go to the Polish army. The cruelty in the army to the Jews was very great and in order to avoid being enlisted he had most of his teeth extracted.

Many Jewish boys mutilated themselves in order to avoid call up. I knew of some who had broken their own fingers or toes, rather than go into the army.

My father also had two sisters. One of them got married before the war. It was a very big wedding and all the family came for miles around. We were up all night celebrating and when we returned home it was already daylight.

Our home was like a meeting place for relations. Whenever there was a Simcha in the family everyone from out of town came to stay with us. My parents would put up thirty or forty people who slept on the floor in our home.

We had many cousins who lived in Lodz. One of them was called Etka (she was the daughter of my aunt Nacha). Etka was a very attractive girl who married Moyshe Kohn. He came from a very important family in Lodz. His uncle was one of the richest Jews in Lodz. He was the owner of a very large factory called Widzewska Manufactura which produced cloth.

Etka and Moyshe were married for ten years but they had no children. Then one morning he walked out of the house and refused to go back to live with her because he wanted to have children.

He wouldn't give her a Get (divorce) and this meant that she could never marry again. As she was still a very attractive young woman she tried everything to make him give her the Get. In frustration she even went to his parent's house and threw stones at their windows, hoping that in this way they would force him to divorce her.

This dilemma was only resolved when her husband's father died and the Beth Din refused to bury him until Etka was given the Get. As she was left on her own she moved in with us and she stayed in our house for many years until the war broke out in 1939, when she went back home to her parents.

In 1941 Etka was taken to a concentration camp with her parents and other members of her family. They all perished except for her. She was lucky to be picked out to work and so managed to survive the war.

We also had a cousin, Gedalia, who stayed at our house. He was born in Warsaw and was a knitting machine mechanic. He used to buy old machines, recondition them and then sell them. Very often people used to call at our house complaining that the machines didn't work.

One day he got engaged to a very pretty girl, whose parents were very rich. They gave him a dowry of 10,000 Zlotys (which was a lot of money in those days), with which he started a knitting machine factory.

They were engaged for a short time, then he broke it off. I don't know why, but I remember his future father in law coming to my parents to ask them to try to get the dowry back from Gedalia. But he had spent most of the money in his business ventures and smart clothing, and buying presents for everybody.

When the war broke out he escaped to Russia, where he met a

young Jewish girl and married her. They had one daughter.

Gedalle had a younger brother whose name was Hershel. He worked for us. One day my father gave him a pile of leaflets that he had had printed to advertise his business, to be distributed.

When I went to visit his mother, who lived not far from us, I went into the toilet and I saw a whole pile of these leaflets. Instead of distributing them he had taken them home to be used as toilet paper.

My father was furious with him and sacked him on the spot. But his mother came round to us later on and pleaded with my father to give him another chance. Which he did.

Hershel was a communist. In Poland at that time it was illegal to be a communist. I remember whenever it was May Day (the 1st of May) the workers used to march in the street. The police used to be on horseback and would arrest the troublemakers and Hershel was always one of those who got picked out. He used to lead the procession as he was the flag bearer. To us children this was very exciting.

Together with his brother Gedalle he ran away to Russia. Hershel being a prominent communist thought that the Russians would make him an official in the Communist Party, but he ended up in Siberia with the rest of the Jews as Stalin suspected them all of being spies. He managed to survive the war but he returned to Poland very disillusioned with communism and emigrated to Canada.

I suppose we were what is now called the middle class. We possessed a telephone and a radio, which in those days were considered luxuries.

We lived in the centre of town at Number 2 Zawadska Street. As it was a corner building it was also Number 13 Pietrowska Street. Our building comprised shops on the ground floor with flats at the back of the shops and on two storeys above the shops.

My parents had one of the shops and sold all kinds of textiles and knitwear. Our shop was situated on the corner of No 13 Pietrokowska Street which was the main street and shopping centre in Lodz. Next to our shop was a grocery store which was owned by our German neighbour.

Entrance to our home in Lodz before the war

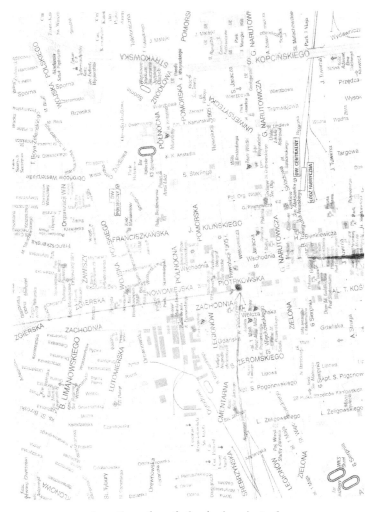

Location of my father's shop in Lodz

All the big firms had branches on that street and some of the shops were owned by international companies. There was great excitement in Lodz when Woolworths opened a branch of their famous department store. It was said you could buy everything there, from a pin to a piano. It was a large building with three of four floors full of different goods.

Opposite our house was a Hotel called The Monopol. There was also a parade of shops including an expensive furniture shop; a shop that sold English worsted material; one that sold hunting guns and a "Kolektura" (a lottery shop). There was also a shoe shop called "Bata" and a hat shop called Hickel.

There was a delicatessen called Diskin. It was a specialist shop and sold all different kinds of Wurst. It was my favourite shop. When I was sent there by my mother it was hard to make up my mind which Wurst to buy – they all looked so delicious.

The shop that sold ice cream was a favourite of my brother Yitzchok. It had an enormous selection of ice creams in different flavours and colours. I suppose it was the forerunner of the American Ice Cream Parlour. The shop also sold halva in a large variety of flavours. Sometimes my brother was in there for ages trying to decide what he was going to buy with the little pocket money he had.

There was a chemist whose window was full of different coloured jars and bottles of all shapes and sizes. Next to this shop on the right-hand corner was a chocolate shop called E. Wedel. This was a beautiful shop with two large windows and a neon lit facia. Many of the shops had neon lighting and at night the street was ablaze with lights in different colours.

When I remember how Lodz was then – bustling and vibrant

with Jewish life; and how it is now – bleak and barren of Jewish culture and tradition; the tears come to my eyes.

All the Jewish shops sold only strictly Kosher food. It is strange that although Lodz had nearly a quarter of a million Jews, there was only one Rabbinical Authority and one Kashrus Commission unlike today.

In the corner of Zachdonia and Zawadcka, which was only 100 metres from where we lived, was a large hotel called 'Mantaufel.' This was a very luxurious building and only the very rich could afford to stay there.

Not far from us was an exclusive Jewish restaurant nicknamed 'Briddiger Shmiel' (Dirty Samuel). It was actually very clean and nobody knew how it got that name.

The entrance to the flats where we lived was through arched gates which led into a courtyard. During the day the gates were kept open. They were closed by the caretaker 11 o'clock at night. If anyone came in after 11 o'clock they had to ring for the caretaker to open the gates and pay him for his trouble. (We didn't have to do this as we could get into our flat through our shop).

When you went through the courtyard there were two or three passages which led to the flats. Our flat was on the ground floor at the back of the shops. It had two bedrooms, one for my parents and one that I shared with my brother. My sister slept on a folding bed which was put up every night in the kitchen. We also had a toilet and a shower. The rents in our district were very expensive and very few families had more than two bedrooms.

Between each room there was a large tiled coal oven which reached from floor to ceiling and warmed two rooms at the same time. It gave out tremendous heat. In the middle of the oven when opened a small door you could keep food or water hot for at least 24 hours.

Our building had very thick walls, about two to three feet thick. The plumbing was in the walls or inside the building, so that the pipes didn't freeze in the winter. After every fall of snow, the caretaker had to sweep the pavement clean. If he didn't do it straight away he was fined by the police.

We also had an enormous basement where we stored perishable foodstuffs such as milk, cream, butter and cheese as well as vegetables and coal.

There was always a lot of traffic passing our house and it needed a policeman at each corner of the junction to direct it. There were trams and horse drawn carriages running through PIetrokowska Street. Outside our block was a taxi rank.

Every summer my father rented a cottage in a village called Kolumna, which was in the middle of a forest; as the air in Lodz was very hot and stuffy and polluted from the big factory chimneys. When one was outside the town and looked down it looked like a forest of chimneys. The smoke belching out from the chimneys was horrendous.

We used to go away a week after Shavous and stay there till a week before Rosh Hashanah. My mother's sister Malka also came with us together with her two boys.

My mother stayed with us most of the time but when she had to go back to Lodz we would have a woman to look after us. My father used to come out for Shabbos. While we were at the cottage he hired a teacher to teach us every day for two hours so that we shouldn't "run wild."

The cottage was near an orchard and we used to help the man who rented it to pick the fruit. As Jews were not allowed to own an orchard or any land in the country they had to rent it from the Poles. We used to look forward to fruit picking every year and although it was hard work climbing the trees to reach the fruit, we wouldn't have missed it for anything.

It was a popular holiday village and was packed with Jewish families. There was a Gerer stiebel and an Alexander stiebel, a Beth Hamedrash and a Mikvah.

The Sochechover Rebbe used to go to Kolumna in the summer, where he also had a Stiebel. The Shabbos service was held in a very large hall, and after the service all the men would come up to him to wish him "Good Shabbos" and shake his hand.

On Friday afternoons my mother used to prepare the cholent for Shabbos. She used a large pot which had handles on each side, and filled it with potatoes, meat and beans. She turned the lid upside down, put potato peels on the top of the lid, covered the pot with a few layers of paper and tied string around to keep the paper in position.

21

She then put a towel through the two handles and my brother and I took hold of each end of the towel and carried the pot to the baker. When we handed it to the baker he stuck a label with a number on the pot and pushed it into his big oven with a long shovel.

On Shabbos morning after shul we went to the baker to collect the cholent. There were usually a lot of adults and children waiting to collect their cholent. It was a big social occasion.

The baker brought out each cholent and a man stood at the side and called out the number that was written on the pot. My brother and myself took hold of each end of the towel and proudly carried home the hot cholent. I still remember the taste.

On Sundays we were discouraged from going outside because there was always trouble when the Poles used to come out of church. They used to beat up any Jew they saw on the street. The Priests of the Catholic Church used to preach anti-Semitism.

My brother and I went to a Jewish school which was the most expensive school in Lodz. As you can imagine with a population of a quarter of a million Jews, Lodz had many Jewish schools. The school we attended was very large and was under the auspices of the Agudas Yisroel. It catered for children from the age of 3 right through to the age of 18. It was very orthodox.

My brother and I started school at 8:30am and we were there till 2:30pm. Then we went home for lunch and returned to Cheder at 4pm and stayed there till 8pm. When we got home (the Cheder was only ten minutes walk from our house) we ate supper and did our homework. We usually had about an hour's homework every evening.

We made the teacher's lives a misery because we were always up to some mischief or other. One teacher was very strict and when he got annoyed with a boy he would pull him up by the ears. Believe me, I speak from experience when I say it was very painful.

We had school every day except Shabbos. We had no rest on Shabbos though, as in the afternoon we had to go to Uncle Shmuel who tested us on the Jewish subjects we had learned during the week. He then had to sign a note after Shabbos so that we could show it to the teacher on Sunday.

My sister went to a state school. At that time, it wasn't thought necessary for girls to learn Jewish subjects. My parents hired a private teacher (Rebbe) who came in every day and taught her how to doven (pray) and how to write a letter in Yiddish.

My father used to take my brother and myself to the Vilker shul on Friday evenings. It contained one of the largest collection of books on the Torah. It wasn't far from where we lived and was always packed with people. Sometime it was so full that people had to stand outside in the foyer.

My father was clean-shaven which was a constant source of embarrassment to me, as all the fathers of the other children wore beards. Although on Shabbos my father wore a "bekisher" and a gartel, as did my brother and myself.

On Shabbos morning we dovened in a Stiebel which was at 33 Pietrokovska Street. It was on the second floor of a large building. My father's father also dovened there.

The Rebbe of the Stiebel was a descendant of the old Ostrovcer Rebbe.

Before Kol Nidre everyone used to light a candle. It wasn't like the memorial lights of today where they burn inside a glass. These candles were put in a bowl that was filled with sand. They were very long and lasted for 26 hours. They gave out a tremendous heat.

On Simchas Torah in the Stiebel we children were given a flag on top of which was an apple, and in the apple was a lighted candle. We danced together with the men who were holding the Sefer Torah. When I look back on it now I'm amazed how we didn't start a fire.

There were many poor people who came to the shul where my father dovened, and every day a different person would pay for their meal. My father once took me to a hall where there were a lot of poor people having a meal. Some of them covered their faces with their hands in order not to be recognised.

Thursday was the day set aside for the poor, when they visited all the Jewish homes and everyone would give them a little money. Before every Jewish Holyday we children were told in school that we must bring some food from home so that it could be distributed to the poor.

I remember there was a blind man who used to be led by a young girl. He called her "his eyes." She always held him by the arm when she guided him and people were very sympathetic and were more generous to him. One day we were surprised to see that he was able to walk by himself. When we asked him what happened to the girl he told us that he had sent her away because she wanted more money.

There was a lot of anti-Semitism in Poland as the government was a fascist one. We Jews did not have many rights. Although there were about three and a half million of us there were only three Jewish deputies in the Sajm, which is the equivalent of the Houses of Parliament in England.

One incident that impressed on me the hazards of anti-Semitism happened when I was 8 years old. My brother and I used to collect the coupons from packets of coffee as these could be exchanged for an album with animal stickers.

When we had collected enough coupons I walked with my brother to the office where the coupons were to be handed in. The office was just outside the Jewish area.

Suddenly a crowd of Polish boys about our age started throwing stones and running towards us. We were frightened they were going to beat us up and we ran so fast that we were soon out of breath.

As children we were always told that if we ever had any arguments with any of the Polish boys we were not to answer back or hit back. This was the mentality of the Jews before the war, to turn the other cheek. This also applied to adults.

One day a builder was doing some painting outside came in to the house and asked if he could borrow a bucket. My mother lent him one which was in good condition. He didn't bring it back so my father went outside to get it and he saw that the bucket had been broken. My father was going to complain to the builder but my mother stopped him as she was frightened if he complained the builder would beat him up.

We lived not far from a market where most of the stall holders were Jews. A young Pole was running through the market with a revolver in his hand shooting indiscriminately at the crowd and killed and wounded a number of people.

A Jewish butcher caught him and unarmed him. He handed him over to the police. There was a big trial which lasted for a long time but the youth was acquitted. This was the kind of justice that we Jews had before the war.

Jews were not allowed to go to University, so if parents wanted their children to study they had to send them abroad. They were discouraged from owning any land or property.

Jews could not start a business without a "Patent" (a licence) and a Trade Guild Certificate, which had to be renewed every year. To obtain the necessary papers one had to enlist the services of a "Macher." He was a person who knew someone in the government who could be bribed to grant a licence or procure other documents.

Everyone who had a shop or any kind of business had to make a regular payment (in addition to the normal taxes that were collected) to help the government buy arms and aeroplanes. My father always grumbled when he had to pay this.

When Josef Pilsudski, the founder of the Polish republic, died in 1935 we all wore black armbands for a week in his honour.

He was officially the Marshall of the Polish army but in reality, he was the leader of the Polish government. He was good to the Jews and while he was alive he kept the others in check so that there wasn't so much anti-Semitism. This was because a Jewish family had saved him when he was in hiding from the Russian Czarist Police.

When he died the government made a film of his life and it was shown in all the cinemas for a week. The entrance was free to all schoolchildren and I went to see the film seven times. There were pictures of him in every shop window draped in the Polish flag as the Poles are a very patriotic nation.

After his death the situation changed. Pogroms against the Jews became more frequent and in 1936 many prominent Jewish business people were rounded up and imprisoned. They were only released on payment of a large sum of money to the Polish government.

There was a well organised Jewish life in Lodz with many schools, Yeshivas and Synagogues catering for all kinds of religious observance. In most Jewish homes the language spoken was Yiddish. There were a few daily newspapers all

27

printed in Yiddish. Some were religious, some were Zionistic and some were non-religious.

Only in assimilated Jewish families was Polish spoken at home. We had to learn Polish in school and every day we had a lesson in the Polish language.

At one time the Polish government was going to introduce a Bill in the Sajm (parliament) forbidding Shechita. As a protest the Jews did not buy any meat from Pesach to Shavous. As most of the meat and chickens were brought from neighbouring farms and as most of the farmers were Poles they were very upset as they lost a lot of business.

The manufacturers of salt also lost out, as the Jewish house-wives used the salt to kasher the meat; so if they bought no meat they didn't need to buy the salt.

Some of the non-religious Jews wanted to buy meat from non-kosher butchers but they were prevented from doing so by Jewish organisations (religious and non-religious) who wanted to show solidarity. As a result the Bill was withdrawn.

All the Jewish shops were closed on Shabbos. When some of them started to be open on Shabbos the Chassidim used to stand outside the shops and stopped the customers from entering.

The main entertainment in our house was a gramophone that we had to wind up and every Saturday evening when Shabbos went out we played Jewish records.

In the 1930's they started bringing in Jewish films from America – The Dybuk, Joseph in Egypt and a Briefele zu der Mama. We had a girl working for us called Fella. She used to take my brother, my sister and myself to the cinema to see these films.

At around this time a large number of Jews were deported from Germany and were dumped on the Polish borders. (They were originally Polish nationals who made their home in Germany). The Poles refused to let them into Poland so they were kept on the border for a long time.

Their plight was written about in all the Jewish newspapers and broadcast on the radio. Many people felt sorry for them as they were treated as refugees and had nowhere to go.

Little did we know what was in store for us and that they were to be envied. Eventually they all got visas to go to different countries, so they were saved the horrors of the Holocaust.

My father wanted to leave Poland and emigrate to Palestine. He discussed this plan with his Rabbi who discouraged him from leaving Poland because in those days people who emigrated became non-religious.

Financially it would also have been difficult because it would have meant selling up everything.

In any case there were many difficulties to be overcome. It wasn't possible for us to get out of Poland without a passport and an exit visa. Just to get the necessary papers we would have had to pay a "Macher" an exorbitant amount of money which was beyond our means. We would also have needed permission to settle in Palestine and the British government only allowed 1500 certificates a month to Jews.

After Hitler moved into Austria and then Czechoslovakia the situation deteriorated. German neighbours with whom we had had friendly relation before started to ignore us.

Many of the Germans living in Poland who sympathised with the Nazi regime started sabotaging bridges and preparing the ground for German occupation. There were a number of ugly scenes and many fights broke out between the Poles and the Germans. Everyone was worried.

The older children of one of our German neighbours disappeared but as soon as the Germans marched into Poland they reappeared wearing uniforms with Swastikas on their armbands

My father remembered that in the First World War there was a shortage of food, so he bought whatever provisions he could and stored them in our basement which was enormous.

He bought sacks of flour, rice, sugar and salt as well as a large lorry load of coal and textiles. Wherever he could find space in the basement he filled it with rolls of cloth.

He spent whatever money he had buying merchandise, as he knew that once war broke out the money would lose its value.

1939

In the summer of 1939 we went away on holiday to the country as usual. When we stayed in the cottage everyone would sit outside in deckchairs (weather permitting) and played the gramophone. We only listened to the radio for the news. All through that summer people were discussing the possibility of war.

Great Britain and France had signed a Defence Pact that if anyone attacked Poland then they would come to her aid. We were all happy that two of the greatest powers in Europe were going to protect us from the Germans.

I remember Hitler giving a speech in Berlin saying he was cancelling the Friendship Pact he had signed with the late Marshal Pilsudski, the Polish leader. At the same time he signed a non-aggression pact with Stalin. So it was clear to everyone that it wouldn't be long before war broke out.

About a week before the war started my father decided that we should return to Lodz from the cottage we rented in the country. (It was about 15 miles from Lodz).

He tried to hire a horse and cart to bring us back without belongings but it was impossible to get one. The government had already requisitioned all transport, trucks, lorries and horses for the use of the army. My father finally managed to track down a Pole who had a horse and cart, and for an exorbitant sum took us all back to Lodz.

Polish propaganda was working at full speed. There were large posters everywhere showing a Polish soldier sticking a bayonet into a German who was depicted as a wild animal.

There were many jokes being told against the Germans and we all hung out the national flag to show our loyalty to the Polish government. My parents also draped a flag in their shop window. Patriotic songs were sung all day on the radio. The air was full of war fever.

There were no air raid shelters but every block formed a defence committee and they selected rooms on the lowest floor of the building, or in the basement, that they thought would be the safest place in the event of an air raid.

Suddenly our Polish neighbours – who up till then had given us the cold shoulder – were on the best of terms with us. This was because we now had a common enemy. Fights between Germans and Poles intensified.

Posters were pasted all over the city asking for volunteers to dig trenches against the anti-aircraft guns. About 50,000 people (according to the Germans) volunteered. My brother and I also volunteered. We used to get home at night with every bone in our bodies aching. We weren't used to the physical labour.

There were also placards on the walls telling all reservists up to the age of 40 to report immediately to Headquarters for general mobilisation.

In the event of a gas attack we were told to take a piece of gauze soaked in bicarbonate of soda, place it in a piece of sheeting, cover the nose and mouth with it and tie it behind the head (similar to the masks hospital surgeons wear). This mask, they assured us, would protect us from poison gas.

My father stuck crisscross strips of paper on the windows in case the glass shattered so no one could get hurt from the fragments. My mother bought blackout material to make curtains.

She also prepared a rucksack for each of us with emergency rations: spare clothing and some money, in case we had to leave home suddenly. We children had to wear an identity label round our neck with our name and address clearly printed on it.

Finally on Friday morning September 1st 1939 the Germany army crossed over the Polish border and entered Poland. On that day we had three air raids. Enemy planes kept flying over Lodz and that night we slept in our clothes.

It was rumoured that the Germans had broken through the Polish front line and the whole civilian population were going to be evacuated. This was in complete contradiction to the news we heard on the radio, which was that Polish troops had repulsed the German attacks, had advanced deep into German territory and had shot down a number of German planes.

On Tuesday night September 5th I couldn't sleep, so I stood with my father on the roof of our building, as he was the fire watcher on duty that night.

Suddenly we heard a lot of noise and we looked down and saw hundreds of Polish soldiers marching on the Pietrokowska Street, which was the main thoroughfare. We were horrified at the sight. Some of the soldiers were barefoot and had been badly wounded. Their legs and faces were bandaged and bloodstained. Many of them were without caps and their uniforms were in tatters.

We realised from the state they were in that they were retreating from the German/Polish frontier, but they pretended that everything was okay.

As my father's shift was finished we all tried to rest for an hour or two, but we didn't undress as we were frightened there was going to be an air raid.

Suddenly, in the middle of the night, someone banged on our front door. "Get up! Get up! Everyone's running away. The Germans are coming."

We all rushed out into the street with our rucksacks. There were people everywhere. Whoever owned a horse and cart had loaded it with possessions. Others not so fortunate had taken as much as they could carry on their backs.

Within a few minutes we were joined by thousands of people all running. Babies were crying, children were in tears, the whole city was in a panic and on the move.

We asked people where they were running but they didn't know. They just wanted to get out of Lodz because the Germans had broken through the front lines and were advancing into Lodz.

We were jostled by the crowds but kept on running for about two hours until we came to the outskirts of the city. We could see the sky lit up with bomber planes. They came down so low we could even see the pilots sitting in their cockpits.

The bombs were falling on all sides and gunners were using machine guns from the planes on to the crowds below. There were dead bodies and injured people lying at the sides of the road as well as many dead horses; also people who were too tired to go any further and were resting.

Then we heard that the Germans were advancing on all sides, so my father decided there was no point in running anymore and we should return home. He said that if he had to die he wanted to die in his own home (and very soon after that's exactly what happened – but that's another chapter).

So we returned home and half the civilian population of the city also came back in the morning. For the next two days the Germans pounded the city with heavy artillery. The noise was unbearable. I was filled with fear and foreboding!

Most of these two days we spent in the shelter in the basement together with our Polish neighbours. We were all terrified that our building would be hit and would come crashing down. Our German neighbours did not join us in the shelter. They kept a very low profile until the Germans came marching in.

We heard later that the Polish army had put up a Second Front near Warsaw and all the Polish troops were converging there. They defended the city of Warsaw for four weeks and made the Germans pay a heavy price for its capture.

On Friday morning September 8th 1939 my brother and I were standing on the corner of Pietrokowska Street which led to Platz Wolnosci, Liberty Square, where the town hall was situated.

In the distance we could see some motor cycles escorting a car which displayed the German flag with a swastika. They drove to the Town Hall and went inside. They were there for about an hour and then we saw them hanging out the German flag, and we realised that this was the beginning of the Occupation of Poland.

Announcements in Polish and in German, signed by the Civic committee of the City of Lodz, were posted on the walls of every building, telling people they had nothing to fear from the German army.

The next morning the German troops marched in to Lodz. They brought with them a band which played military music. The street was lined with Germans who were hugging and kissing the soldiers and throwing flowers.

We were also standing at the side looking on. To us children the procession was cheerful and exciting. Little did we realise the significance of the scene we were watching.

Later that same day two German soldiers knocked on our door. They wanted to know who owned the shop which sold hunting guns. When my father told them, they demanded that the owner open the shop; then the soldiers brought a lorry and emptied the shop of all the firearms.

In sharp contrast to the Polish soldiers the German soldiers were smartly dressed. They occupied the Hotel Monopol which was opposite our house.

After a few days there was a shortage of bread and there were long queues outside the bakeries. The Germans picked out the Jews from the queues and wouldn't let them get served. So my mother went out and bought my brother and myself the same school caps that the non-Jewish boys wore, in order that we shouldn't be recognised as Jews. Otherwise we would have had to buy bread from the Poles who would have sold it to us at a much higher price.

My father didn't dare to stand in the queue, as he would have been too conspicuous. Cutting off, or plucking out, beards of the Orthodox Jews in front of jeering crowds was a favourite pastime of the German soldiers.

Sometimes for additional amusement they shaved off only one half of the beard, leaving the other side of the face smooth. Then these Jews had to walk with a scarf tied around their faces to hide their shame from their neighbours.

One day our neighbour, a Mrs Berkovitz, came running into our apartment crying. My mother tried to calm her down as she sobbed that her husband went out to try and get some bread and he hadn't returned. She dreaded to think what might have happened to him.

The next afternoon her husband returned and he told her that he'd been standing in the queue and the Germans came along and picked him out. They took him into a large room. There were already a number of Jews there. Some of them were wearing beards. The Germans beat them and kicked them and cut off their beards.

Then a man entered the room wearing a white overall. He took out one of the Jews and we heard terrible screams coming from outside. We were all terrified.

Soon after the German came back into the room. He was holding a large knife in his hand which was full of blood. One by one the Jews were taken out and beaten up. But no one was killed.

Later we were told that the blood was from killing chickens. The Germans were having a laugh at our expense. The whole charade with the knife was just to frighten us.

The Dayan of the district where we lived was Rabbi Yossele Feiner. One Shabbos morning we saw him passing in an open car flanked by two Gestapo officers. He was wearing a Tallis. They took him away and beat him up. He returned a few days later a broken man. He could withstand the beatings but the mortal sin of desecrating the Sabbath was more than he could bear.

In Lodz, in 1939, no mass killings had yet taken place. Now and again they would swoop down on an unsuspecting Jew and shoot him. Either because he was rich and he wouldn't hand over his money to the Gestapo or just for the fun of it.

It was getting dangerous for Jewish men to walk in the street. They were easily recognisable because they dressed differently and wore beards. So they were picked up from the street, herded into halls, and never heard of again. People alerted each other "Don't go out" but it was very difficult.

Then the Jewish leaders made a deal with the Germans that they would select 700 people (mainly men) every day for work, if the Germans would stop picking people up from the street.

The Germans agreed to this but of course they didn't keep to their side of the bargain and they still made indiscriminate and frightening roundups of Jews.

It was rumoured at the time that we would have to leave our apartment and the Germans would take it over for themselves. They had already evicted Jews from some of the most elegant apartments. They tried to provoke the rest of us to leave the area, by putting more and more restrictions on the Jews.

The Germans forbade us to walk in Pietrokowska Street which was the main thoroughfare and had the most expensive shops and apartments.

All the Jews who lived in the apartments in Pietrokowska Street had to buy specials passes to allow them to walk in the street. These cost ten marks each per week for each member of the family.

The passes only allowed the Jews to pass through Pietrokowska Street to get to other places – it didn't allow them to walk down the street.

We didn't need to buy these passes as the house we lived in was on the corner of Pietrokowska Street and Zawadska Street. So we were able to go out and come back whenever we liked.

We heard that the Germans had rounded up a number of Poles who had been caught dealing in black market goods. They put some gallows in Zielony Rynek and the Poles were hanged in full public view, together with a few Jews who were also involved.

Gradually the Germans changed the names of all the main streets and Pietrokowska Street became known as Adolf Hitler-strasse. For some time the Jews had been forbidden to print any of their newspapers and now the Poles were also not allowed to publish any of their newspapers.

It was coming up to the High Holydays. It was the first Rosh Hashana that we weren't able to daven (pray) in Shul, as the Germans had locked up all the Synagogues. People were too frightened even to organise a minyan of a few men to pray together in their own houses in case the Polish or German neighbours would report them to the Authorities.

Caretakers of every building were ordered to make up a list of all the Jewish tenants in their block.

In the weeks that followed, the Germans organised the Jews to do the dirty jobs – cleaning the streets, clearing the rubbish and cleaning their cars. They accompanied their orders with kicks and beatings.

Every day they issued notices (Bekanntmachung) which they hung up on every street corner. One said that no Jews were allowed to be out in the street from 5 o'clock in the evening to 8 o'clock in the morning; and they were not allowed to use public transport or be seen in public places such as cinemas or theatres.

In October 1939 the Jews were ordered to hand in all their valuables, jewellery, fur coats etc to the police stations in each district. They were warned if they didn't obey this order they would be severely punished.

The Jews, and also the Poles, were also ordered to hand in their radio sets so that they couldn't hear broadcasts from foreign countries.

In November an edict was issued saying that all Jews, irrespective of age and sex, must wear a yellow Star of David just under the shoulder at all times, sewn on the back and front of their clothing.

Jewish shops had to display a sign stating that the owner were Jews. Jewish bakeries were forbidden to bake or sell any cakes, biscuits or any confectionery, other than bread.

All the Jewish schools were closed down and the Germans sealed up the buildings with large heavy padlocks so that nobody would be able to reopen them.

Although the Jews kept to all these restrictions they were nevertheless ordered to leave the city, as the German announced that Lodz had to be "Judenrein" (free of Jews).

The Germans arrested thousands of professional people: including teachers, doctors, engineers and lawyers. They were taken into market halls and from there they were sent away never to be seen again.

In large Jewish firms the Germans installed a Kommissar. This was one of their own people whose job was to oversee the work, report back to the Authorities and to check on stocks and accounts. Once the Germans understood how the business was run they ordered the Jewish owners to stay away and they ran the business.

Poznansky owned the largest textile factory in Eastern Europe. It was one of the companies that the Germans took over. He was very wealthy and was a great philanthropist. He built the Jewish hospital in Lodz.

Poznanki's Mausoleum in Lodz

People tell me that the Lodz Town Hall is housed in one of the Poznansky Palaces he had built for his family. Even today when one visits the Lodz Jewish cemetery one can still see the elaborate marble mausoleum built by the descendants of the Poznansky family.

Towards the end of 1939 the Germans started destroying all the shuls (synagogues) in Poland. In Lodz there were many beautiful shuls but the three main shuls were each famous in their own right.

My father used to take my brother and myself to the Vilker shul on Friday evenings which was not far from where we lived. My grandfather (my father's father) also davened there. The Vilke shul was famous because throughout the day and night there were always groups of men and youths studying Talmud in the building.

This shul contained one of the largest libraries of books on the Torah. It had a dome that towered over all the surrounding buildings and could be seen for miles.

Then there was the Temple. It was considered a Reform shul as it was built by "enlightened people" who wanted a modern synagogue with an organ. It was situated on Kosciuszko Street which was in the centre of town.

The oldest and most beautiful shul was the Old Town Synagogue. It was built by Italian master craftsmen and workers who were brought over specifically for this purpose. Poznanksy donated an enormous amount of money towards the building of this

Synagogue and the decoration of the interior.

Wielka Shul

It was a very tall and imposing building. It could seat 1500 people. There were two women's galleries, many Torah scrolls and silver ornaments, as well as antique works of art.

Whenever there was a national holiday or other official occasion the governor of Lodz and many Polish generals would take part in the ceremonies there.

When the Germans came into Lodz they confiscated the keys to all the Synagogues. Early in November 1939 they gave the keys back to the representative of the Vilker shul and ordered him to arrange a New Year's service complete with cantor, choir and a person to blow the shofar (ram's horn).

The Shul was packed with congregants who were forced to attend and were made to wear talleysim (prayer shawls) and tefillin (phylacteries). Cantor Winograd conducted the service accompanied by the choir. They sang a selection of prayers from the Rosh Hashanah (New Year) service and from the Yom Kippur (Day of Atonement) service.

Then the German officers, who were filming the entire service, ordered that the Torah scroll be taken out of the Ark so that the Reader could recite the weekly Portion.

The next day a similar incident took place in the slaughterhouse. The Jews were ordered to slaughter a number of cattle and recite the appropriate blessings. This was also filmed by the Germans for their archives as Hitler had planned to document these events in a 'museum of an extinct race.'

On Wednesday night in the middle of November 1939 the Temple on Kosciuszko Street was burned to the ground. All the Torah scrolls and interior fixtures were destroyed. On the following night the interior of the Old Town Synagogue was destroyed by fire, together with all the Torah scrolls, silver ornaments and antique works of art. The building was dynamited.

Some months later the Germans set fire to the interior of the

Vilker shul. Tens of thousands of rare books were burned and the Torah scrolls were removed. To this day nobody knows their whereabouts.

Chanukah (the Festival of the Lights) arrived. My father tried to cheer us all up by telling us that our troubles would soon be over. When he lit the first Chanukah candle I remember we all huddled together away from the window so that no passer-by could see the candles burning.

It warms my heart today when I light the Menorah and place it in front of the window for everyone to see the candles burning.

In December 1939 Germany declared that Lodz was to be annexed to the German Reich and was to be known as Litzmanstadt after General Litzman who was killed in the 1914-1918 war while fighting to gain control of Lodz.

The Germans decided to speed up the evacuation of all the Jews from Lodz as they wanted the whole of the German Reich to be Judenrein.

The town of Opatov where my cousin Etka came from was not included in the German Reich. It was in the Polish Protectorate and was not annexed; so my father decided that we should move to this town from Lodz while there was still time.

He hired a horse drawn lorry and we filled it up with all our worldly good: clothes, books, furniture, pots and pans etc. We went very slowly as the load was heavy. When we got out of town we were stopped by two Folksdeuschen (ethnic Germans) who were dressed in black uniforms with a swastika on their arms. They ordered us to follow them to the Police Station.

My mother was frightened that my father would get beaten up so he quickly climbed down from the lorry and ran away.

When we arrived at the Police Station they told us to unload the lorry and bring everything into the station. There they opened every case and every box we possessed and inspected the contents; then they took most of the stuff for themselves.

My father had packed many of his Hebrew books in the lorry. To my amazement one of the German officers opened one of the books and started reading from it in Hebrew. He began to pour scorn on the Bible.

"This Moses," he declared, "this leader of yours, he was a bastard. They found him in the river and they didn't know who his parents were." He continued to taunt us in a similar vein all night.

In the morning they let us go and told us to take the few possessions they had left us and to load them on to the lorry. We journeyed for two days until we reached Opatov. My father joined us soon after and we stayed there for a few weeks.

It was very difficult to live in Opatov because of the overcrowding. Lots of people came in from other towns which had been annexed to the Third Reich. My parents, my brother, my sister and myself had no proper place to sleep and food was becoming scarce.

As we had a full cellar with food at home and there were rumours that things were quietening down in Lodz and that the situation had improved, my father decided we should return home.

Once again, he managed to get hold of a horse and carriage to take us back, although he had to sell most of our belongings to get German marks for us to live on, as Polish zlotys were worthless.

1940

In January 1940 the German government announced that they were going to form a ghetto in Litzmanstadt, formerly Lodz, for the Jews to live in. Instead of the Jews having to leave the city, they were going to be moved to accommodation in selected streets in the poorest part of town.

A detailed plan and outline of the Ghetto was published in the Litzmanstadt Gazette. According to this plan it would take nearly two years to move a quarter of a million Jews into the ghetto, as the German and Polish inhabitants living in this area would have to be rehoused.

In February 1940 the Germans started moving the Jews into the Ghetto, street by street. After a few weeks they could see that this would take too long so they had to find other means to speed up the process.

On Thursday afternoon 7th March 1940 my mother went to the market as usual to do the weekly shopping. When she arrived home she said that on the way back from the market there were more German soldiers that usual in the street. I looked out of the window and saw a number of German soldiers surrounding our building.

I told this to my father who suspected the worst. He said we should quickly put on our overcoats, as it was bitterly cold, and take our rucksacks. As we were doing this two soldiers banged on the door and shouted to us "You have 15 minutes to assemble downstairs in the yard. Anyone still found in the building will be shot on sight."

As the soldiers left our flat we heard shots being fired. We thought they were warning shots to make us hurry up so we quickly ran out on to the communal staircase. The soldiers grabbed my father and pushed him back into our flat. Then they pushed us down the stairs into the yard.

As we came into the yard I saw a woman lying in what I thought was a heap of red snow. When I came nearer I could see that she had been shot and had been bleeding profusely in the snow.

The German soldiers pushed us into the arch where the gate was and as we stood there shivering with fright, with our rucksacks on our backs, we heard more shots coming from our building. We couldn't believe that the shots were being fired in cold blood against people for no reason.

The courtyard of our building

After about half an hour of shooting more soldiers came down from the apartments and we saw that they were from the SS, as they had the skull and bones insignia on their helmets.

We were marched out into the street. There were no civilians to be seen but every few yards a soldier stood with a gun pointed at us. They kept hitting us with the rifle butts so that we should drop everything that we held in our hands.

We marched for about two hours into the renowned Balouty Slum. This was the area that was to be established as a Ghetto. It had not yet been cordoned off, but according to the plan that we had seen in the Litzmanstadt Gazette we knew this was going to be the Ghetto. Then the SS handed us over to the Jewish police.

The Jewish police was organised by a man called Chaim Mordechai Rumkovski. Before the war he was in charge of a Children's Home. He was also a member of the Geminno (the Jewish Council). He had no children of his own but he had experience in organising.

When the Germans entered the city of Lodz they tried to get in touch with the leaders of the Jewish community but most of them had run away and were in hiding. Rumkovski, therefore, was appointed by the Germans to be in charge of the Ghetto.

Within months every Jew in the Ghetto would be familiar with his name. His full title was The Elteste der Juden in Litzmanstadt (The Elder of the Jews of Litzmanstadt). He was very proud of this role. He was an autocratic and despotic leader and extremely ambitious. He thoroughly enjoyed the power bestowed on him by the Germans.

Many people thought it was wrong of Rumkovski to co-operate. Others were of the opinion that if he hadn't things would have been much worse for the Jews. We will never know who was right.

That night we were taken to an empty school building and we stayed there for two or three hours. Then the Jewish police announced that whoever had relations living in the area could leave. My mother decided as she had a brother (our Uncle Shmuel) living not far from where the school was, we should go and stay with him.

My uncle had a wife and four children and they all lived in one room; so as you can imagine it was very difficult for us to stay there.

On Friday the 8th March 1940, the day after the mass shooting of the men and women (including my father), over 150,000 Jews who were still living in the city ran into the Ghetto. They were frightened there would be a repetition of the indiscriminate shooting of the night before. There was chaos in the streets.

Many Jews ran away from the city and managed to get to Russia. My mother was too upset by the murder of my father, and having three young children to look after, to think of escaping to Russia. Perhaps if we would have done, she and my sister would still be alive today.

People left their apartments and took with them as much as

they could carry on hand drawn sleighs. People were dressed in as many layers of clothing as they could wear so that they could put as much as possible in sacks to carry on their backs.

The snow was thick on the ground and progress was slow because the Jews were not allowed to use public transport. The Poles and the Germans looked on laughing, as the Jews tried to drag all their belongings into the Ghetto.

When we looked out of the window of our room it was a most pitiful sight that met our eyes. We could see old people shuffling along, some were leaning heavily on sticks, as well as blind people being led by the hand.

There were mothers carrying screaming babies in their arms whilst the other children were carrying bedding and clothing in their arms. In their panic they dropped things on the ground which were soon trampled on.

That same morning my mother and sister went along to the offices of the Jewish leadership, which were at No 6 Kosceilna Platz (Church Square) and tried to find out what had happened to my father and to the other men.

There were already a lot of people there who were in the same position as my mother. After waiting a long time they managed to see Rumkovski.

"My heart goes out to you all," he said. "I promise you I will find out what happened to the men and if the worst that I feared has happened I will see that the bodies are returned for a decent burials." This he never managed to do and to this day I don't know where my father was buried.

My mother and sister were heartbroken when they came back to us. We didn't have to ask them what they had heard at the office; one look at their faces told us the tragic news.

A week later Rumkovski sent two Jewish policemen and two German policemen with my mother to our home to get us some warm clothing; as in the rush to vacate the apartment we hadn't been able to take any change of clothing with us.

When she asked the Polish caretaker what had happened that night he started crying and wouldn't say anything. She told us there was no sign of the carnage that had taken place, no blood on the landings or in the yard – to the casual observer everything looked normal.

A few days later two badly injured men had returned to the Ghetto. They said that all these men – as well as some women (800 people in all) had been shot in cold blood that night. It was later referred to as 'Black Thursday.' It was the first pogrom in Lodz.

The bodies of the dead had been loaded on to lorries and driven away out of town. Pits had already been dug and the bodies were thrown in these pits. Wherever there was a movement of life soldiers attacked them with bayonets to make sure they were dead.

Somehow these two men escaped from these death pits. They

hid from the soldiers and managed to get back to the Ghetto. Once they were in the Ghetto they were seen by doctors and taken to a hospital for treatment.

We were still sharing the room with my mother's brother and his family, but eventually my mother managed to get a room in a large block of flats which we had to share with my father's brother and his wife.

We separated the room with a curtain. As there were four of us (my mother, sister, brother and myself) we had the largest part of the room. In our part there was only space for two beds. I slept with my brother and my sister slept with my mother.

There was a small table in the middle of the room. When we used to eat at the table we had to sit on the beds, but we considered ourselves fortunate as many others were living ten to a room.

There was no water in the room. We had to use the pump to draw water which was some distance away. There were no toilet facilities except for a hole in the ground which was also quite far away.

Our apartment building in the Ghetto

My mother couldn't get used to these spartan living conditions. She also felt out of place with our new neighbours who gloated over the fact that it was a comedown for us to live in these slums, where crime was rife and hardened criminals used to roam the streets.

One man in particular that I remember was the caretaker of our block. He was a cripple with only one eye and although he only had one leg and had to walk with crutches, he terrorised the neighbourhood.

His 20-year-old son took a fancy to my sister Rachel, who was 16 at the time. She was very beautiful with long auburn hair and he was always pestering her.

It only took a few days for all the Jews to gather in the Ghetto. Many people had to sleep in the open – despite the intense cold – until the Germans and Poles who lived in the Ghetto were evacuated to the City, to occupy flats that the Jews had been forced to vacate. Unlike the Jews they were able to take all their possessions with them.

When the Ghetto was closed a lot of Christians stayed behind. There were two sorts of Christians: one sort were born from Jewish parents although they didn't want to be known as Jews. There were no churches in the Ghetto.

Then there were other Christians who could have left the Ghetto and could have stayed with the Poles. Some of them had married Jewish partners and others had been servants in Jewish homes and did not want to be separated from them.

Finally the Ghetto was enclosed with a barbed wire fence. Hundreds of German guards patrolled outside armed with guns; while the Jewish police were marching inside to stop the Jews going too near the fence. Nobody could go in or out without permission. We were the outcasts of society – made to feel like lepers.

After the Ghetto was fenced in there was an acute shortage of food as no deliveries were allowed in. Whatever food was available was very expensive.

In May 1940 it was announced that Jews were not allowed to leave the Ghetto. This also included the leaders of the Ghetto and the Jewish police.

Entry into the Ghetto by Germans or Poles was strictly forbidden, unless they had special identification cards signed by the Chief of Police. If they did have to go into the Ghetto, before they left they had to go through disinfection centre, in order not to spread diseases outside.

A few weeks after the Ghetto was closed the Germans authorised Chaim Rumkovski to open a bank. Everyone was ordered to bring in all foreign currency that was still in their possession, including German marks. These were to be exchanged for special paper money that was printed in the Ghetto.

Ghetto Money

On one side of the note was a picture of Rumkovski and his signature, and on the other side was a picture of Moses holding the Ten Commandments. This money was only valid in the Ghetto. After collecting all the foreign currency and German marks he handed them over to the Germans in exchange for food.

When all the currency was used up Rumkovski realised that the only way for the people in the Ghetto to survive was to work to produce goods; and with the money he received from the Germans he could buy food.

So he put forward a plan to the German authorities that they should allow him to set up factories in the Ghetto. There were many skilled people who could manufacture merchandise that the Germans needed for the war effort. At the same time it would keep people off the streets.

The German authorities gladly accepted the proposal and Rumkovski – who was an excellent organiser – with the help of some of the Jewish leaders set up a number of different factories.

There were about 12 thousand tailors in the Ghetto so these were the first factories to be set up. Then there were factories producing metals, munitions, cloth, household textiles, carpets, shoes, ladies and gents' hats and leather saddles for horses.

There were also workshops that repaired sewing machines and from the fur coats that were handed in by the Jews, trimmings were made for the officers' uniforms.

There were a lot of large buildings that had been sealed up by the Germans and were not allowed to be used by the Jews, such as cinemas, churches, schools and many public buildings. Rumkovski persuaded the Germans to open them up so that he could use them as work places and to store materials and food stuffs.

There was a hospital in the Lagiewnicka Street which had accommodation for 400 beds. As it was empty he transferred the patients of the Poznanski hospital, which was situated outside the Ghetto, and this building was used to treat the Jews.

Every block was ordered to set up a committee to be responsible for the cleaning of the building, as well as the yard and the street. The Ghetto became an autonomous city within a city with its own currency, police force, fire brigade and medical service. They even printed their own newspaper.

The Germans, being very methodical, ordered Rumovski to make a list of all the people living in the Ghetto. He had to supply a comprehensive list, giving details of every man, woman and child and their ages. Every week he had to make out a similar list of all the people that had died in the previous few days.

Surname	First name	Sex	Birth date	Occupation	Address	No.	Notes
JZ KUPELNICKA	PRIMELA		/ /1904		SIEGFRIED 39	13	FNE 0.0.43
JZBAUM	CHANA	F	/ /1886		SIEGFRIED 39	13	
JZBAUM	CHAWA RUCHLA	F	/ /1915		BLEICHER 6	26	
JZBAUM	DOBA	F	/ /1916		SIEGFRIED 39	13	
JZBAUM	ESTERA	F	/ /1919	ARBEITERIN	SIEGFRIED 39	13	STEIN 7
JZBAUM	FAJGA HINDA	F	/ /1911	SCHNEIDERIN	STORCHEN 12	9	STORCHEN 12 A.G. 10.7.44
JZBAUM	FAJGA HINDA	F	/ /		AGE IN 1940: 28		
JZBAUM	GITEL	F	/ /1901		AM BACH 15	42	
JZBAUM	ICEK	M	/ /		STORCHEN 12	10	AGE IN 1940: 29
JZBAUM	JEHUDA ARJA	M	/ /1924		SIEGFRIED 39	13	
JZBAUM	LAJA	F	/ /1932		BLEICHER 6	26	
JZBAUM	LAJB	M	/ /1923		SIEGFRIED 39	13	
JZBAUM	MENACHEM	M	11/2/1944	KIND	BLEICHER 6	3	
JZBAUM	NACHMAN	M	/ /1935		BLEICHER 6	26	GEST 29.8.42
JZBAUM	PESA MALA	F	/ /1912		SIEGFRIED 39	13	
JZBAUM	RYWKA	F	/ /1926	SCHUSTERIN	SIEGFRIED 39	13	STEIN 7
JZBAUM	SZAJNDLA	F	/ /1914		SIEGFRIED 39	13	
JZBAUM	SZLAMA	M	/ /1937		BLEICHER 6	26	A.G. 11.9.42
JZBAUM	SZMUL	M	/ /		STORCHEN 12	10	AGE IN 1940: 6 MIES
JZBAUM	SZMUL JANKIEL	M	/ /1939	KIND	STORCHEN 12	21	MASARSKA 12 AUSG SEPT 42
JZBAUM	TAUBA MALKA	F	/ /1922		SIEGFRIED 39	13	
JZBAUM	URYSZ BER	M	/ /1884		SIEGFRIED 39	13	
JZEN	JOSEF	M	27/1/1909		HOHENS 4	9	REMBRANDT 12
JZER	RYWKA	F	15/10/1905		AM BACH 15	63	AM BACH 15
JZEROWSKI ?	ZACHARIA	M	/ /1910	SCHNEIDER	BLATTBIN 5	3	ZGIERSKA 92 GEST 25.3.43
JZKA	ZEFTEL	F	26/1/1925	ARBEITERIN	CRANACH 21	16	OZORKOW ABG 12.1.44 CRANACH 2
JZLER	SURA	F	10/3/1910	ARBEITERIN	INSEL 26	100	LAGER 31 A.G. 23.6.44
JZMAN	ABRAM FISZEL	M	24/1/1912	SCHNEIDER	KELM 79	3	ALEXHOF 8 AUSG 26.2.42 TR 5/2
JZMAN	ABRAM SZMUL	M	/ /1903	SCHNEIDER	AM BACH 31	11	KILINSKIEGO 17 GEST 5.11.42
JZMAN	AJDLA	F	6/5/1921	ARBEITERIN	BLATTBIN 24	1	WLOSZEWO
JZMAN	ALEKSAND DAWID	M	15/10/1926	SCHUELER	HOLZ 37	27	ZIETEN 2 ABG 23.6.44 HOLZ 16
JZMAN	ALTA	F	5/10/1912	BUROANGEST	HANSEATEN 9	38	SULZE 32 ZAM 19.11.41
JZMAN	ALTA	F	5/10/1922	BUROANGEST	SULZF 33	5	GEWERBE 70 GEST 24.10.41
JZMAN	AWRUM FISZEL	M	/ /1912		ALEXHOF 8	33	
JZMAN	BERNARD	M	1/7/1928	SCHUELER	INSEL 35	21	MITTEL 57
JZMAN	BERNARD	M	1/7/1928	SCHUELER	INSEL 35	21	MITTEL 57
JZMAN	BLUMA	F	/ /1933		SCHNEIDER 18	15	STEINER 16 AUSG 19.3.42 TR 23
JZMAN	BLUMA	F	10/12/1939		SCHNEIDER 18	16	
JZMAN	BRANDLA	F	/ /1916	ARBEITERIN	HAMBURG 8	8	
JZMAN	CHAIM	M	/ /1869		ALEXHOF 8	33	
JZMAN	CHAIM	M	/ /1869	WASCHEREI	KELM 79	3	ALEXHOF 8 GEST 17.2.42
JZMAN	CHAIM JOSEF	M	/ /1906	BUROANGEST	HOHENS 40	19	
JZMAN	CHAIM JOSEF	M	/ /1903	BUROANG	HOHENS 40	12	PRZ DOM 19
JZMAN	CHAJA SARA	F	20/12/1934		KORB 15	5	AUSG 20.5.42 TR 11/2
JZMAN	CHAJA SYMA	F	15/9/1927	SCHUELERIN	KRANICH 13	4	GANSE 2 AUSG 22.2.42
JZMAN	CHANA	F	/ /1910		ALEXHOF 8	41	
JZMAN	CHAWA RUCHLA	F	14/11/1914		ALEXHOF 8	33	
			26/11/1936	HANDELSSCHULE	KELM 79	3	ALEXHOF 8 AUSG 26.2.42 TR 5/2

Alexsand Dawid Rajzman on the Ghetto list

In the summer of 1940 conditions in the Ghetto deteriorated. Food became very scarce and the overcrowding was intolerable. There was also the danger of epidemics breaking out.

Trouble started erupting in the streets as people realised that the Ghetto was completely cut off from the outside world. They started demonstrating in the streets and a number of riots broke out.

Rumkovski ordered the police to pick out the ringleaders who were imprisoned and then later sent away. So with the leaders out of the way things gradually quietened down.

At the beginning of 1940 Rumkovski announced that the Germans wanted 700 people for work outside the Ghetto. As there was a shortage of food and money and work inside the Ghetto wasn't yet so well organised, many people volunteered as they thought that in this way they could help their families.

At first, they sent money and letters to their families. My two cousins who lived near us used to send money to their mother (my aunt) for a few months. Then suddenly all communications stopped and we heard no more from them.

Even in the Ghetto we were not allowed to walk in the streets before 8 o'clock in the morning and after 5 o'clock in the evening. The only exceptions were the police, doctors and other medical workers.

It was some time before Rumkovski was able to obtain permission for the curfew to be eased, when we could be in the streets from 7 in the morning till 8 o'clock at night.

The Ghetto was divided into three parts and was intersected by two important streets, the Zgierzie Street and the Novomienska Street. No pedestrians were allowed to walk on these two streets. Only German and Polish trams, buses and horse drawn carriages were allowed access.

On each side of these two streets were high barbed wire fences which were patrolled by German guards. Every 50 meters there was a guard armed with a machine gun.

In order that the Jews could cross from one side of the Ghetto to the other without holding up the German traffic the Germans built three wooden bridges. They cost 20,000 marks each to build and this had to be paid by the leaders of the Ghetto.

There were always long queues of people waiting to cross over. It was quite dangerous at times, as the guards used to shoot indiscriminately at the people who were crossing.

I remember one incident when I crossed the bridge. A guard was shooting in the air and the man in front of me fell down, and he looked as if he was wearing a red mask. This was because he had been shot in the face and he was full of blood.

The Bridge in Lodz Ghetto to get from one side of the Ghetto to the other side

By the summer of 1940 all our valuables had been exchanged for food and we had no more money left. Then my mother received a letter from Rumkovski offering her work.

She was still distraught from the shock of my father's death and too weak from lack of food, so she asked if my sister (who was 16 at the time) could take her place.

So my sister, Rachel, started work in a Co-operative which was a store where they distributed the food rations. She wasn't allowed to take out any food from the premises but she could eat while she was at work.

Bread was strictly rationed and was only available in exchange for coupons. It was very dark and heavy and weighed about 2kg. The daily ration varied from 250gm to 400gm depending on the amount of flour available in the ghetto.

When we collected two days bread ration from the Co-operative it was the equivalent of a quarter of a loaf. So the distributors could steal a small slice of bread from each loaf. Thereafter Rumkovski ordered that the loaves should not be cut and they should be distributed whole in order to avoid any more stealing.

The trouble was that when a person received a week's ration of bread all at once it didn't last the whole week because people were so hungry that they ate it in three or four days. My young brother Yitzchok could never make his bread last the whole week so my mother used to share her ration with him.

When the bread was delivered from the bakeries to the Co-operatives to be distributed, each horse drawn wagon was attacked by the starving crowd. So every delivery had to be guarded by two Jewish policemen armed with long truncheons.

There were terrible scenes about the lack of food in the Ghetto. People became like wild animals. I shall never forget the time when a father took the loaf of bread from his son and when the boy protested and tried to take it back the father strangled him with his bare hands.

In the Winter of 1940 an epidemic of typhoid broke out in the Ghetto. There was no running water in our block and my brother and I took it in turns to bring in buckets of water from the public pump which was quite a distance away. More often than not the pump was frozen up. There was also no proper toilet facilities.

Apart from the lack of food there was no fuel available for heating or for cooking. People became desperate and they started pulling down fences and cutting down trees to use as firewood.

Although the Ghetto police warned that anyone found stealing fences or cutting down trees would be severely punished nobody took any notice. Soon there were no more fences and no more trees left.

There were many houses built of wood in the Ghetto. It became dangerous for the people living in them to go out work during the day and leave their houses empty, as on their return they were met by a shell of a building.

People descended on the houses like vultures and in no time at all everything that could be used for firewood had been pulled to pieces and carried away.

As my father was one of the first victims, and Rumkovski had promised my mother he would look after us all he arranged for her to get a sack of coal every month which we collected from a central depot.

During the next few months thousands of Jews were deported which gave more space in the Ghetto. At the time we never realised that these people were being killed. We were told that they were being resettled.

All the families that lived in wooden houses were rehoused into brick-built buildings. What was left of the wooden house soon disappeared.

1941

I n the spring of 1941, when I was 14 years old, I started work in a factory in Lagiewnicka Street that had been opened up specially for boys. We had adult overseers and I was taught how to use the sewing machine. I still remember the feel of the thick heavy cloth that was used for the soldier's uniforms.

I started work at 7 o'clock in the morning and finished at 6 o'clock in the evening. Everybody was given a bowl of soup at work. Sometimes the soup looked like dirty water with half a potato swimming around in it, but we were thankful for it.

We worked 6 days a week in the Ghetto and the first time I worked on Shabbos (the Sabbath) I thought my hands would fall off. It took many weeks before I got used to the idea and stopped feeling guilty.

Rumkovski used to show off with our factory to the Gestapo, because he made use of the youngsters who produced goods for the war effort.

I used to get paid for my work in the factory with ghetto marks. We could use this money to pay for our rations but if we wanted to buy goods on the black market this money wasn't worth much.

In order to earn money to get food, my brother and I used to buy packets of tobacco on the black market. When I came home from work in the evenings we rolled cigarettes to sell in the ghetto. We did the same with saccharins.

When my grandmother died mainly from hunger I couldn't attend the funeral as I wasn't given the time off work. To this day I don't know exactly where she was buried. I know it was somewhere in the cemetery in Lodz.

They had mass graves at that time, because they had so many bodies to bury every day. They used to collect these bodies on carts which were pulled along by the Jews as there were not enough horses available.

A few weeks later my grandfather also died from hunger. He had been a fine figure of a man, tall and strong. He had served in the czarist army. He used to tell me stories how strong he was when he was younger.

At the beginning when we went into the ghetto we were given a ration of half a pound of horsemeat a month, but nobody would touch it as it wasn't kosher. Then after months of near starvation we were only too glad to eat it as we were getting weaker and weaker.

Rumkovski established a special commando unit in the police to deal with troublemakers. They use the same methods as the gestapo and were very ruthless. The troublemakers were sent to one of the prisons in the ghetto and were the first ones to be deported by the Germans.

Rumkovski testing soup in the Ghetto

In the middle of May 1941 we heard through the underground radio that Churchill gave a speech in London. He said that England had suffered major defeats and although it looked as though the war would continue for a long time, England would fight until victory was theirs. This speech didn't give us much hope that we would be able to survive.

In July 1941 all the mentally ill people were rounded up and deported. Also, one day in July, when I looked out of the window from our block I saw that the streets were completely deserted of people. There were a lot of cars full of SS officers on the way to the gestapo headquarters in the ghetto. This was because Himmler was going to visit the ghetto.

To prepare for his visit the streets were cleaned and scrubbed and we were ordered to whitewash everywhere so that every-thing should look spick and span.

We were all very frightened as we didn't know what Himmler was planning for us. But one thing we did know, that it wasn't going to be anything good.

Himmler congratulated Rumkovski on the way he organised everything in the Ghetto. After this, Rumkovski ordered that his own picture should be hung up on the wall of every shop, office and factory.

A few weeks after Himmler's visit the Germans started sending in able-bodied men and women from the small towns around Lodz. The old people and the children from these town were sent away – nobody knew where. There were rumours going around that the Germans had set up concentration camps but we had no proof.

In the Autumn of 1941 different transports of Jews were arriving in the Ghetto from all over Europe, having been deported from their countries. They came from Germany, France, Belgium, Austria, Luxembourg and Czechoslovakia.

As the newcomers got off the trains they were shocked at the scene that met their eyes. We were living skeletons having been under German occupation for two years with the minimum of food.

Our clothes were shabby, while these men wore smart suits and the women were elegantly dressed with fashionable hair styles. When they saw the appalling conditions under which we lived and the filth and the squalor they were horrified.

The luggage they had brought with them, clothes, bedding and goods were put on horse drawn wagons and was taken away. It was stolen by the local residents and by the Jewish police.

The Germans had told these European Jews that they were being sent to Jewish autonomous region, with Jewish police, where they would be well housed and well fed. They had been promised good jobs in their own professions as they were very educated.

They told us that when they'd been put on the trains in their home town their travelling conditions were good. However, as soon as they reached the Polish border they were transferred to Polish cattle trucks and were beaten up by the Polish guards.

At the beginning the newcomers refused the bread and the soup and gave it away, which was eagerly seized on by the rest of us. But after a few days when they became weak and hungry they were glad of the rations.

When you're hungry food becomes the most important thing in your life and it didn't take longer than a few weeks for these professional people – doctors, scientists, lawyers, architects etc – to fight with their bare hands along with the rest of us for any food they could get.

They tried desperately to get work however menial, as they realised that without work they would be sent away. Those that survived started selling off their possessions for the bread they had once spurned.

I had frost bite in my feet and it was painful to walk in the wooden clogs, and I remember getting a pair of black shiny shoes from a doctor, in exchange for my ration. They were too big for me but I padded them out with newspaper which eased the pain a little.

Of the 50,000 people who entered the Ghetto at that time from other countries, half of them died within 6 months. These were mainly the older people and children, as they weren't used to living under such dreadful conditions. We were already acclimatised to the overcrowding, starvation and lack of sanitation.

In October 1941 about 5,000 gypsies arrived in the ghetto. The Germans cleared two streets near where we lived to accommodate them, and surrounded the area with barbed wire. It was called the gypsy camp.

The Gestapo used to beat the gypsies unmercifully. We used to hear blood curdling screams coming from there. Dead bodies were regularly piled up in the streets. This gypsy camp lasted for about a year, then it was closed down and the gypsies that were still alive were deported.

The Gypsy Camp

My mother together with some other women were sent to this camp to clean up after the gypsies. My mother used to come home every evening sobbing at the atrocities she saw that had taken place. She found plaits of hair from women that had been wrenched out from their heads, as they still had a lot of flesh on them.

Up till this time there were still one or two places set aside where the older men could sit and learn the Talmud. Then Rumkovski ordered that these places should be closed down. He also ordered that all the men should shave off their beards and wear short jackets, as he was frightened that the Germans would see these Chassidim and make a lot of trouble.

A special prayer was composed by some of the Rabbis to be

recited in the few clandestine synagogues that still existed in the Ghetto then:

"*May it be Your will to hearken unto the heartfelt sighs and pleadings that come from our hearts each and every day, evening, morning and afternoon. Our endurance is under strain. We have neither a leader nor a source of support, nor anyone to turn to and rely on, save for you, our Father in Heaven. Merciful Father, You have visited upon us a daily torrent of retribution, famine, fear and panic. At morning we ask who will provide for us at evening, and at evening we ask who will provide for us at morning. No one knows who among Your people Israel will survive and who will fall victim to plunder and abuse. Unlock our shackles and remove our tattered, befouled clothing. Return to their homes those who have been abducted, captured and deported. Our Father in Heaven, we beg you to restore sons to their mothers' embrace and fathers to sons. Have pity on them and protect them from all afflictions wherever they may be.*

Lead us from darkness to great light so we may serve You with all our hearts and souls. Help us to keep Your holy Sabbath and festivals joyously and with great delight.

May all who seek refuge with You experience neither shame nor disgrace. May you speedily bring peace to the world and stifle evil wind that has come to rest upon your creatures.

Around this time all the school were closed down. Although Rumkovski promised that it would only be a matter of time before they were re-opened, they never opened again.

In the winter of 1941 there was an outbreak of tuberculosis in the ghetto, and thousands of Jews died from it. Also, because of the insanitary condition typhoid spread like wildfire.

My sister, Rachel, was also a victim of the typhoid epidemic. She had very high fever which is the first symptom of typhoid. She also had strong headaches and pain in her abdomen.

We were told by the doctor that it is highly contagious and so my sister was taken away to hospital, where they shaved off the hair on her head and body. There were no drugs available so we didn't expect her to come back alive. My sister survived typhoid, only to perish later on in Auschwitz.

As it was so contagious we were put in quarantine and were not allowed to leave our rooms for three weeks. There was a policeman standing outside to make sure that we stayed inside.

We were only allowed to go out to fetch water and the policeman went with us to make sure that we didn't mix with any other people. He used to shout to them to keep away from us, and he pumped the water himself, in order that the water shouldn't get contaminated.

Towards the end of 1941 the Gestapo started making lists of all the people in the ghetto who were not working. Caretakers in every building were ordered to hand in a detailed list of everybody, including the old people and the children.

In December 1941 my uncle and aunt, who had shared their room with us in the ghetto, were picked up by the police in the middle of the night and were sent away. We just kissed them goodbye. Although it was heart-breaking to part from them, we couldn't even find the tears to cry.

About 30,000 people were picked up like this and sent away. They were supposedly going to be sent to work but nobody believed it, and they were never seen or heard of again.

Rumkovski at this time was about 60 years gold and to everyone's surprise he married one of his secretaries. He made a big party and invited all the leaders to join him in celebrating his wedding.

1942

The year 1942 was the blackest and most tragic year for the Ghetto. The deportations increased daily. Rumkovski warned that more sacrifices would have to be made. His favourite phrase was "We must cut off a limb to save the body."

The Ghetto population at this time was about 162,000 people, which included Jews that came in from West European countries. The Germans said it was impossible to feed so many people as there was a shortage of food so more deportations would have to be made.

In January 1942 Rumkovski ordered all the people who had come into the Ghetto from Western countries to report at certain assembly places for deportation.

"Those who do not register voluntarily," he thundered, "will be collected by force. Don't think that you can hide. Wherever you hide you will be found. I am warning you all not to let anyone into your home who is not registered at your address."

He continued: "Should any persons who are approved for

evacuation be found in the homes of other families, not only will they but also their families and the house watchman be sent out by force. This is my last warning to you all."

In February we were all ordered to assemble in the Fisch Platz. It was called by this name because before the war the fishmongers used to bring in their catch here to sell to the public. Thousands of people turned up. We were all given time off work to attend.

Then Rumkovski gave a speech in which he announced that the authorities had asked him to deliver 700 to 800 people a day for deportation. He said that these people shouldn't worry. Nothing bad will happen to them. They are being sent into the country to work on farms.

He also ordered all the people who were not working to register. Then the police started searching houses for the people who were not working to take them to the assembly places.

As they went into the houses to look for people they found many children and old people starved and frozen to death. Even the mice were laying in the middle of the room, frozen, next to rags and old shoes.

Rumkovski giving a speech in the Ghetto

The people had been too weak to light a fire and, in any case, they had had no fuel.

The price of a loaf of bread shot up to 100 marks. A kilo of margarine also cost 100 marks. As the deportations continued the price of foodstuffs spiralled because the deportees sold their possessions to buy food to take with them.

In the factory where I worked we were too dispirited and too weak to carry on. As we looked out of the window we could see the people who were being deported rushing backwards and forwards with their bundles on their backs.

One bitterly cold day in the middle of February 1942 we were again ordered to assemble in the Fishchplatz. We were not given a reason but we heard rumours that a military parade was going to take place.

Sick people were permitted to be absent. The men were told that they should take places in the front and the women in the back.

By 9 o'clock in the morning the square was filled with 20,000 people. Then a gallows was erected by the Jewish police. Some of the women fainted as they looked at this macabre sight and others started weeping and wailing.

A few well-fed German officers stood by smiling. At every exit from the square soldiers were stationed with machine guns to keep the crowd in check and to see that no one escaped.

We stood there for over an hour in silence. From the Baluter-ring, which was the Gestapo headquarters, a man with grey hair came out flanked by German soldiers. When he caught sight of the gallows he stumbled and had to be supported by the soldiers.

There was a deathly silence. We were all frightened to breath and although it was bitterly cold, nobody dared to cough or make the slightest movement.

The German soldiers were warmly dressed and wore fur coats. They took off the overcoat the man was wearing and pushed him to the front of the crowd and up the steps to the gallows. He folded his hands and looked around at the crowd as he mounted the steps.

There was still a deathly hush as they hung the noose around his neck. Suddenly we heard a dull thump of a heavy plank of wood falling and within a few seconds all we could see was a body twitching in the air. They left the body hanging on the gallows the whole day.

Later on we learned that the night before, the Building Department had been ordered to erect a gallows by 7 o'clock the next morning. The job was given to a German Jew who had to work through the night to get it finished in time. When he saw that the condemned man was his intimate friend he later committed suicide.

The percentage of Jews that committed suicide was much higher among the Jews who arrived from Germany or other Western countries. They couldn't acclimatise themselves to the harsh conditions in the Ghetto.

In March 1942 Rumkovski gave another speech – he enjoyed giving speeches – as he was a very fine orator. He said: "I am opening new factories and I expect everyone in the Ghetto to be employed. Whoever doesn't work will be deported but everyone who is working in the factories will be entitled to collect extra rations."

On the way home from the factory it was not unusual to see policeman dragging old people into lorries and driving them away to be deported.

The streets were full of snow and ice, and bodies of people who had dropped dead from cold and hunger. Men were employed to collect the dead bodies and take them away in lorries to be buried in mass graves.

Rumkovski also announced that a new road was going to be built from the Ghetto to Maryshin. This was the railway depot where all the supplies in and out of the ghetto were handled. This road was also the way to the cemetery and to the railway for the people who were being deported, but this he didn't tell us.

Whenever a new ration was distributed, I rushed to the Co-op after work to collect my rations. There were always such long queues and crowds of people that it was difficult to breathe. The people were covered with lice and I tried to stand against the wall so that the lice wouldn't get to me.

We hoped that when the weather became warmer the famers would open their underground stock piles of potatoes and there would be more food available.

The deportations stopped temporarily and the ghetto was suddenly flooded with potatoes. People had not seen a potato for weeks and because they all bought potatoes, the price of bread on the black market halved.

One Saturday morning in April 1942 the postman delivered two letters to us. When we saw the postman with these two letters our hearts sank. In the Ghetto they were called "Wedding Invitations."

One letter was addressed to my mother and the other to my younger brother Yitzchok. My sister and I didn't get a letter because we were both working. They were orders to report at the Assembly place for deportation.

After she read the letters my mother wrote to Rumkovski. She reminded him of the promise he gave her in March 1940 when my father – who was one of the first Jews to be shot in Lodz – that he would always look after us. She implored him to take her name and my brother's name off the deportation list.

The next morning she got up very early and went to the place where she knew his carriage would pass on the way to his office. It was an open horse drawn carriage travelling at a very high speed, and as it drew near my mother threw in the letter. This frightened the horses and they nearly killed her.

She could see that one of the men who were sitting with Rumkovski in the carriage picked up the letter and opened it. A few days later a note was delivered to us by hand, dictated and signed by Chaim Rumkovski. He wrote that he had given the matter a lot of thought and he was prepared to allow one person to be freed. In other words, either my mother or my brother would have to be deported.

After a heart-breaking discussion it was decided that my younger brother should be the one to be deported; as he was young we hoped he would be able to survive. Also, we still hoped against hope that deportees were sent to work and were not being sent to their death.

Yitzchok packed his rucksack with clothes and some provisions, and in the morning, I walked with him to the Assembly Point where he had to report. I kissed him goodbye but there was not time to say anything more than a few brief words.

That same day about noon when I was at work in the tailoring factory we heard an unusual noise in the street. We all rushed to the window and saw crowds of people laughing and cheering in the street. Then we heard that the deportations had stopped.

The relief was tremendous and I quickly got in touch with my mother. She and my sister had already been told the news but they were worried that the news had arrived too late to save my brother.

About two or three hours later my brother came running back to us; we were all very happy and this time I kissed him with joy in my heart. The joy of having my brother back with us unfortunately didn't last very long.

A week or two later an order was issued that all the people who were not working had to be examined by a Special Commission of doctors who were sent in by the Gestapo. After the examination, the doctors stamped on their body's certain numbers and letters in indelible ink. Nobody knew exactly what these numbers and letters meant.

Soon after this order went out, people started queueing at the Employment offices to get work – any kind of work. My brother and my mother also queued up. My brother managed to get a job in a metal factory. My mother also managed to get a job in a depot sorting used clothing.

There were wagon loads of clothing coming in every day to the factory. We couldn't understand where it was all coming from. Later on we learned that this clothing was taken from the people who were deported and sent to the gas chamber.

One day my mother came home in tears. When sorting out some clothes she'd found a note in one of the pockets. It was written by a man who had recently been deported. He wrote that he was standing in a long line of people waiting to go into the gas chamber. He realised that he wouldn't come out alive and so he'd written the note as a warning to others.

Towards the end of May 1942 thousands of Jews who were still alive were rounded up from the little towns around Lodz. They weren't given time to take any of their belongings with them and were herded on to cattle wagons and brought into the Lodz Ghetto.

These Jews knew more of what was going on that we did, as in the little towns they still mixed with the Poles. They told us that the Jews who had been deported from the Lodz Ghetto had all been told to undress as they were going to have a bath and to fold their clothes neatly in a pile.

While they had undressed, they were pushed into specially built airtight lorries. The lorries were then sealed and these Jews were gassed with the exhaust fumes from the lorries. This took place in a town called Chelmno, which was situated near a large railway junction.

Postcards were received by many families in the Ghetto, written by people who had been evacuated months before. They were very cheerful and told their relations that they were working on farms, were well looked after, and had plenty to eat.

It was much later when we found out that in actual fact these people had been killed months before the relatives had received the postcards from them.

Whenever the Germans wanted people to volunteer for deportation they cut food rations so that the hunger became unbearable. People queued for hours outside public kitchens for potato peels and even for these peels we had to produce a doctor's certificate. A certificate was only granted to people who had swollen legs.

In the summer of 1942 a tram line was built. It ran from the Platz Koschielna through Lagiewnicka Street to Marishin, which was on the outskirts of the Ghetto near the railway line.

A few weeks later large consignments of worn shoes from men and women arrived in the place where my mother worked. The heels had all been torn off. The Germans suspected that the Jews had hidden valuables in the heels, such as diamonds and foreign currency. The shoes were all sorted out into pairs and then sent to the leather factory to have new heels put on.

Around this time Rumkovski received an order from the Gestapo requesting him to find out if there were any machines capable of grinding bones in the ghetto, as these were needed by the Special Command Unit in Chelmno. Later we learned that they would be used to grind down the bones of the people who were burned in the crematoriums.

In June Chaim Rumkovski gave a speech. He said that although there was a population of 130,000 Jews, only 100,000 were employed. If these 30,000 didn't find work they would be deported. He intended to open new factories to get as many people as possible to work.

All the children over the age of ten managed to find work. Special factories were opened for them to be trained for useful work. We all believed that if we worked this would save us from being deported, and for the next few weeks it was quiet.

Sometime in July Rumkovski announced that he had to deliver 25,000 Jews under the age of ten and over the age of 65 to be deported. He set up a committee to compile a list of all the people who came within this category.

However, on the 4th September 1942 events took a turn for the worse. We assembled in the Fire Brigade Square where Chaim Rumkovski spoke to us. He said: "A painful blow has struck the Ghetto. We are being asked to deliver the best that we possess – our children. I never imagined that I myself would be called upon to ask you to deliver this sacrifice."

He continued: "In my old age I must stretch out my arms and say brothers and sisters, mothers and fathers, give me your children. Yesterday afternoon the Germans gave me the order to select 20,000 from the Ghetto, otherwise they will do it themselves.

They originally requested 24,000 children but I pleaded with them to accept 20,000. They agreed but only on condition that they will be children up to the age of 10. Children over the age of 10 are saved."

He wept like a child as he said: "This is the most difficult order

I have ever had to carry out. Give into my hands your children, hand them over to me, so that we may avoid having further victims. The Germans promised me that if we deliver them there will be peace and the fate of the remaining 100,000 Jews in the Ghetto will be safe."

There were heart-breaking scenes in the Ghetto over the next few days, as the Jewish police tore the babies and young children from their mothers' arms. The children of the Jewish police were allowed to go free. There was no justice in the Ghetto.

We all aged years in those few days. The fear and heartbreak was contagious. All of us felt that we were candidates for the grave. We knew that only a miracle could save us and our loved one, but in spite of everything we all wanted to live.

I remember a young neighbour of ours holding the hand of her little four-year-old daughter. The SS officer told her to let the child go. She said: "I can't be separated from her."

He replied: "I'll give you two minutes to change your mind, otherwise I'll shoot you both."

She thought he was bluffing when he told her to face the wall. Still clutching the hand of the child she turned to face the wall.

He then took out his revolver and with just two shots they were both dead. We were all shaken by this episode.

In the ten days that followed, incidents happened to us that I shall never forget. I was working in a tailoring factory at

Lagienwicka Street 36. There was a hospital opposite at number 37.

One morning we looked out of the window and saw trucks drive up to the hospital, and out jumped Police, Gestapo and SS men. They ran into the building and a few moments later all the windows were opened wide. Then the air became full of bodies which they threw on to the trucks like bundles of dirty washing. Old people, young people, children. Their screams of agony haunt me to this day.

In the evening when we left work we were told that we shouldn't report at the factory until further notice. The next day a curfew was announced forbidding anyone to leave home.

Although we were terrified by the curfew, we were still hoping that we would not be deported as officially the deportations only applied to children under 10 years of age and people over the age of 65. So we felt fairly secure as we were all working and my mother at the time was only 42 years old.

But the day after the curfew was announced, when we looked out of the window from the room where we lived, which was on the second floor, we saw Germans and Jewish police in the yard. As they entered the yard they fired shots in the air, and with a loud hailer they called out: "Everybody must assemble in the yard immediately. Whoever is not downstairs in five minutes will be shot."

As soon as we heard this we picked up our rucksacks and ran downstairs to join the other people who were already standing there. An SS officer was there and started selecting people in two lines. We could see that one line was for those who were to die at once. The other line was for those who would live in torment a little longer.

He picked out my mother and my younger brother Yitzchok in one line, and my sister and myself on the other. My sister didn't want to leave my mother, so she joined her on the other line. I didn't want to stay on my own, so I also joined my family.

We were put on horse drawn lorries and were driven out on to the main road. The roads were completely empty of people, apart from the SS who were driving around in cars and motor cycles.

As we passed the fish market we saw about 30 gallows with people hanging on them. The SS were sitting drinking and laughing and looked at us as we passed. We were terrified. Nobody dared to utter a word.

Finally we reached a hospital on the Drewnoska Street. It was originally an isolation hospital used for people who had infectious diseases. It had a very high brick wall around it with glass and barbed wire on top. As we entered the gates we heard bloodcurdling screams and shouts from people trying to escape from the building.

The hospital was surrounded by very large grounds and the Jewish police were trying to push everybody from the lorries into the building. We tried to avoid this and we managed to stay in the grounds as it was getting dark and we hid in the bushes.

We stayed there all night. During the night it was quiet. The Germans didn't bring in any new people and they weren't taking out anyone. But towards the morning the traffic started again.

They had rounded up new people from the Ghetto during the night and brought them into the hospital. From the other side of the building we could see lorries rounding up these people and driving them away outside the Ghetto.

We already had a good idea what was going to happen to us and to the people who were being deported. The way they handled the old, the ill and the young, we could see that these people were not being sent to work.

We decided we must escape so every time the gates opened bringing in lorries of people from the Ghetto a crowd of people who were inside tried to push themselves towards the gates to get out.

The hospital on Drewnoska Street

As we were also trying to push our way out of this compound we saw a policeman. His wife used to work for us before the war. When he saw my sister Rachel he said he would help her escape. He managed to get hold of a white overall with a red cross. Then he put her on a lorry that was used for medical staff that was about to leave.

Then the same policeman, who was on duty near the gates, saw my mother pushing through the crowd and he let her go through.

So I was left with my brother inside.

We saw that everyone was helping each other to get over the wall. They were standing on each other's backs to be able to get to the top.

So I got hold of my brother Yitzchak, and with the help of the other people I lifted him up and he jumped over. Then I was also lifted up and helped to jump over. It was a very high wall and as I fell down I couldn't get up.

Then I heard shots being fired from all directions and I don't know from where I got the strength, but I started running away. The shots seemed to be following me. I ran for about ten minutes over open fields until I reached the blocks of the Ghetto.

Right through the period when we were in the Ghetto, in order not to be walking on the main roads where we were in danger of being picked up by the Germans or the police; the people had broken through the walls from one building into the other. This meant that one could go from one block into the other without having to go through the main road.

So I ran from one block to the other until I finally reached the street and the block where we lived. There was not a soul about and I went up to the room where we lived. I sat in the room and waited. I had nowhere else to go. I didn't see anybody and I didn't know what to do, so I just saw down and I waited.

When it was dark my mother turned up and then my brother and then my sister. We sat together in the dark because no one was supposed to know that we were back. We didn't know what was going to happen to us.

The next morning when we got up we heard noises in the block and we saw that some people had managed to get back the same way we did.

There was nothing to eat. Whatever food we had in the room had been stolen by the people that the Germans left behind. We sat like this for the next two or three days not knowing what was going on in the streets. All we could hear was sporadic shots being fired. They were coming from the main road.

We decided if they do come for us again we wouldn't go down. Whatever was going to happen let it happen in our rooms. So we made arrangements to hide. My brother would himself in a large trunk and the rest of us would go up on the roof of the building and stay there.

My brother was told that before he went into the trunk he should put a padlock on the hatch so it will look as if nobody is on the roof.

Two days later there were noises in the yard. We looked out very carefully so that we wouldn't be seen from the outside. We saw Gestapo coming with the Jewish police. They started shooting in the air and shouted through the loudspeaker: "Everybody who is still in the building should come down. They should not be frightened. If the come down peacefully they will be given a loaf of bread and a bowl of soup."

This was always their weapon to lure people to the assembly places. They knew everyone was hungry so they promised they would give them a loaf of bread and plenty to eat.

The Germans, to encourage the Jewish police to help them round up the Jews, promised that they would spare their relatives and children from deportation. They were also offered supplementary food rations.

So we set our plan into operation. We went up to the roof and my brother hid himself in the trunk. Then we heard the Germans come into the building. They ran up the stairs and they looked everywhere in the rooms, but they didn't come up to the roof.

They went into the room where we lived and they looked around everywhere. They opened the cupboards but they didn't find my brother and they went away again.

After half an hour it quietened down. We came down from the roof but we stayed in the room. We didn't make a sound so we shouldn't be heard from outside. Two or three days later the curfew was over and we heard people moving about in the streets.

In that week about 24,000 people were deported. As there were now less people in the Ghetto, the Germans ordered that the Ghetto be reduced in size. So a few streets were taken away and the fence was moved inwards.

The Germans had already planned to make a part of the whole area of the Ghetto when the Jews would be finally liquidated.

The shpero (curfew) changed things dramatically in the Ghetto. The autonomy that Rumkovski enjoyed until now was gradually reduced. The Germans had a more direct influence on the day to day running of the Ghetto. They came in more often to the factories to see what was going on and gave orders direct to the factory managers.

All orders and proclamations had to be in German, not in Yiddish as before. They were now signed by the German Ghetto Administrator, Hans Biebov.

Up to this time there was still a Rabbinate in existence, consisting of a few Rabbis. When the shpero was over the Germans forbade the Rabbinate from officiating at marriages. Later we learned that all the Rabbis had been deported.

You might wonder why, living under such conditions, people wanted to get married. It was because they were lonely, and marriage gave them hope for a future. Although they had no food and no heating, two people could somehow manage better than one person on their own. Rumkovski tried to perform the ceremony according to Jewish law.

1943

I n 1943 the mood in the Ghetto was more and more sombre. Nobody smiled, everyone was frightened. Short of a miracle we knew we were doomed. There were no children in the Ghetto – only little old Jews.

The overcrowding and cramped conditions in the Ghetto were almost unbearable. There were approximately 130,000 Jews packed into an area of 4 square miles.

So many people died from hunger and disease that it was impossible to bury them with proper funerals. The bodies were collected from houses in handcarts, and buried in communal graves.

The Nazis seemed to have succeeded in their intention to create such dire conditions that made it impossible for any human being to survive.

One thing constantly occupied our minds – Food! The symbol of the Ghetto was the pot. Everyone had one. From the people who emptied the rubbish, to the VIP's. People waited for hours to have their pot filled. Fear was a constant companion.

I remember seeing a man who had sewn a diamond in the lining of his jacked giving it to a guard. In return he was given some rotten potatoes. The man grimaced and said: "This is truly the Stock Exchange of Hell."

Everyone was terrified of falling ill, as all sick people were deported. So we turned up for work, even though we had a fever and could hardly stand on our feet. The managers of the factories were ordered to report all sick people to the doctors.

All the young children who were still allowed to stay alive in the Ghetto, like the children of the police, were ordered to register. Rumkovski promised that they would be looked after by trained nurses in kindergartens. But nobody believed him and they all tried to hide their children.

Enormous consignments of used clothing were still coming into the warehouse where my mother worked. We realised these clothes had been taken from people who had been deported. In the pockets of some of the clothes my mother found various documents: letters, ID cards and photographs that the Germans had overlooked. My mother was forbidden to tell anyone what she found.

In April 1943 we heard there had been an uprising in the Warsaw Ghetto. Some Jews had managed to arm themselves to resist deportation.

The Germans were forced to use tanks and machine guns, even bombers, to quell the trouble. Then the Germans had set the Warsaw Ghetto on fire.

Notices appeared in the streets that the authorities were aware that German newspapers were circulating in the Ghetto. "Anyone found reading such a newspaper, or having one in their possession, will be severely punished."

An order was issued that every worker must carry an identity card with a photograph to be shown on demand.

Nearly every day, high ranking officers came into the Ghetto to inspect the factories. There were rumours that the Red Cross were going to send in food parcels and fresh clothing, but we soon realised that these rumours were unfounded.

1944

In the beginning of February 1944 Rumkovski gave a speech in the House of Culture. This was a place where concerts were given for the ghetto hierarchy. Rumkovski said the German authorities wanted him to deliver 1,500 healthy men to work outside the Ghetto. Not many people reported but eventually they were picked up at night and dragged from their beds.

In March 1944 there were still 80,000 Jews living in the Lodz Ghetto. Most of these didn't originate from Lodz but were sent in from all the little towns that had already been made Judenrein.

The deportations continued, and although our rations were increased slightly, food was now not the main worry on our mind. Terror reigned in the street. People warned each other "Don't go out otherwise you too will be deported."

A lot of shady deals took place in the factories around this time. The leaders of the factories had to give in lists of names to the Gestapo of people to be deported. In order to avoid deportation Jews used to bribe the leaders either with money or with valuables not to include their names in the lists.

Some Jews volunteered to be exchanged for other Jews. Their price was three loaves of bread or margarine or sugar; or items of warm clothing.

What we found very worrying was the fact that the trains went out packed with people and after four or five hours the trains returned empty.

In the summer of 1944 the first Allied air raids started. It gave us all hope that the war would soon be over and we would be saved. As we looked through the barbed wire that surrounded the Ghetto we rejoiced to see hundreds of German soldiers marching in disarray away from the front line.

Later we heard that the Russians had reached Warsaw and occupied half of Poland. The Poles had staged an uprising in Warsaw. We could hear the sound of heavy gunfire in the distance.

The Allied air raids increased. We could have got killed, but we prayed that the raids would continue. We preferred death from the allies' bombs to starvation or deportation by the Germans.

Sometime in July 1944 Hans Biebov, Chief of the German administration, ordered everyone who was working to come to listen to him. We all assembled in the Fisch Platz, which was the largest square in the Ghetto.

He began his speech with the words "Meine Juden." We were all surprised at the mild tone of his voice. "As the front is coming nearer the ghetto must be evacuated. All the factories and all the machinery has to be transferred to Germany."

He said he had no intention of splitting up families and provided we registered voluntarily no harm would come to us. He assured us that the living conditions in Germany were much better than in the Ghetto. But nobody believed him and very few people reported.

So the Jewish police picked up people at random on the streets and made night raids on the houses so that they could get their daily quota of people who were to be deported.

The tailoring factory where my cousin Alter Metzker worked was ordered to report to the assembly place. (Alter lived with us after his parents and his brother were deported in the 1942 Spero). My mother begged him not to go but he didn't listen to her. He picked up his rucksack which was already packed with his essentials and he kissed us all goodbye.

A few days later the people in the factories where we worked were ordered to report to the assembly place. We didn't go. Instead we decided to go into hiding. We had to keep moving from place to place to avoid being picked up by the Jewish police.

Chaim Rumkovski and Hans Biebov in the Lodz Ghetto

We also faced other difficulties. We had no good reserves, no rations and no running water. At night either my brother or myself would go to the water pump which was some distance away. My mother was always frightened that we would get caught.

Because of the regular deportations, the part of the Ghetto where we lived gradually emptied of people. The Germans wanted to clear this part and they ordered the remaining Jews to report to the assembly places, otherwise they would be shot on sight.

So at night the four of us crossed over to the other part where my aunt lived, and moved in with her and her three teenage children. Her husband (my uncle Shmuel) had died from hunger a long time before in the Ghetto.

One morning we heard that the Germans had surrounded the block. They were going from room to room, together with the Jewish police, to take out the people for deportation.

Under the floor of our room there was a pit where coal used to be kept. It was covered over by floorboards and there was a bed on top. The eight of us went down into this pit. We were practically laying on top of each other and could hardly breathe.

The Germans came into our room. They saw our rucksacks laying around. We heard one of the Germans say: "They must be somewhere around, because here are their rucksacks."

They redoubled their efforts to find us and we could hear their footsteps walking overhead. Our hearts were beating so loudly that we were sure they would hear us; but finally they gave up and went away.

All we had to eat was ersatz coffee which kept us alive. It was physically impossible for the eight of us to stay in that room much longer. Nearby there were empty rooms from people who had been deported. So my mother decided that we should move over to one of those empty rooms to give ourselves a breathing space.

We stayed in that room until we ran out of water. Then my brother Yitzchok took a chance and went to the water pump. As he was pumping the water he was caught by the Germans. He wouldn't tell them were we were hiding but they beat him up so badly that he had no choice and he came back with the Germans.

We were terrified that they would beat us up or shoot us, but instead they escorted us to the tram, which was not far away. The tram took us to the railway station, which was on the outskirts of the ghetto at a place called Marishin.

When we arrived at the railway depot there were thousands of Jews there. We were herded on to cattle trucks and pushed around like animals. There were about a hundred people on each wagon. Everyone was given a loaf of bread. Then the doors were closed.

The windows, and the cracks between the boards, were sealed from the outside so that we couldn't see where we were being taken.

There was barely any air coming into the trucks. The stench was horrendous from the urine and excrement. We stood crammed together for about five hours, until it got dark. Everyone was exhausted from standing so long, and many fell down and were trampled on. Then the train started moving and we travelled all night.

In a way we felt relief that hopefully our ordeal was over. The strain was beginning to tell on all of us and I didn't think that we could take much more. We had had nothing to eat in all the weeks we had been in hiding, and we were fed up of running from one place to the other like hunted rats in a trap. We realised that we wouldn't be able to hide ourselves any more.

In the morning the train stopped and as we looked through a tiny crack in the board we could see men dressed – in what looked like to us – like striped pyjamas. We stayed in the train for about two hours.

Suddenly we heard dogs barking. The doors were flung open and we were ordered to "Get Out!" We could hear shouts of "Schnell! Schnell! Schnell!" as we scrambled out.

As we fell down the Germans started hitting us with their rifle butts to get us moving quickly. Whoever didn't come out straight away was dragged out by the Germans and beaten up.

The people who were unable to walk were picked off the wagons and thrown like sacks of potatoes on to waiting lorries and were driven away to certain death.

I later heard that these people were taken to a place and each one was shot in the back of their necks and thrown in a large pit.

A short time later when we stopped, we were ordered to throw down our rucksacks and were pushed along a ramp. A man whispered in my year in Yiddish: "Wenn men fragt dich, sug du bist achtzehn" (Say you are 18 years old if they ask your age). I didn't realise at the time what he meant by this.

My brother asked him the name of the place where we were and he answered: "This is Auschwitz!" I asked "What's so special about Auschwitz?" and the man answered "You'll soon find out."

Auschwitz

When we arrived at Auschwitz the men and the women were separated. My mother and my sister Rachel were taken away with the other women and I was left with my brother. My mother's last words to me were: "Look after Yitzchok."

We soon learned that Auschwitz was a place where death became a way of life. It was the end of the journey through the Gates of Hell to the death factory for us Jews. It was supposed to have been the final grave of a race that was regarded as being unworthy of life. I travel back there every time I go to sleep.

The next morning we had to queue up in front of an SS officer who was standing with a whip in his hand. As he scrutinised us we straightened ourselves up and held our heads high so that we should look older.

He motioned with his whip that we should go to the right. We were pushed along with the others to a building that had a sign outside 'Badeanstalt.'

When we saw this sign we were filled with terror. We had heard rumours that people were taken to a bath and then gassed, and we were sure that was going to be our fate.

We were pushed into a tunnel in the building and in the tunnel we were told to strip except for our shoes and to leave our clothes behind. Then we were rushed into a room where barbers shaved off our hair – not only from our heads but also from our bodies.

We were made to run along another tunnel that had a foot of chloride in it. It was very painful as when we ran it splashed and burned our bodies. After that we were taken into a shower room. I remember looking up at the shower head and thinking: "If it is gas, please let me die quickly."

After we had showered we were driven out like cattle, and beaten on the head by the Sonderkommands. We saw stacks of different shades of hair which had been brutally torn off from the women before their heads were shaved.

Gold teeth and dentures grinned grotesquely from the piles of false teeth. All kinds of spectacles from expensive horn-rimmed frames to cheap glasses were collected and put into piles. I imagined the eyes that had stared terrified through these glasses before they were ripped from their faces.

We were pushed into a pre-fabricated wooden barrack where we were issued with a thin striped jacket, trousers and a cap and ordered to put these clothes on.

As we were marched out from this barrack I could see a group of women passing. Although they all had their heads shaved I recognised my mother and my sister. I was happy as I realised that they were still alive, but I never saw them again!

I learned after the war from my female cousins what had happened to my mother and to my sister Rachel. My mother was picked out for the gas chamber but my sister didn't want to be separated from her, so they went to the gas chambers together. This happened around Rosh Hashana so I commemorate my mother's and my sister's Yahrzeit on the first day of Rosh Hashana.

All the time the Germans fired shots in the air to frighten us and they kept shouting "Schnell! Schnell!" Their vicious dogs kept barking without a stop.

We were squashed together into another barrack all day without anything to eat or drink. In the middle of the night the Gestapo came in, each one held a torch in their face. They picked out people at random and frightened them by shining a torch in their face. One by one they were led away, then we heard shots being fired.

They shouted: "Anyone who has swallowed diamonds or hidden foreign currency in their shoes should come forward voluntarily. Everyone will be x-rayed and if we find anything that has not been handed over to us the person hiding them will be shot." Many people came forward and were led out.

When it started to get light in the morning the gates of the barracks were opened. We were all pushed out and beaten, to the accompaniment of the barking dogs. We were told to form lines of five. We stood like this for about two hours. It was bitterly cold being so early in the day and all we had on was the thin striped uniform.

We were in the main part of the Auschwitz concentration camp called Birkenau. It consisted of flimsy wooden huts with leaking roofs, crowded with bunks which housed about 100,000 inmates.

Every transport that was sent to Auschwitz from all over Europe arrived here first. Birkenau was the place where the crematoriums and gas chambers were sited.

Those fit for work were selected on one side but the majority were sent to the gas chambers. The Gestapo counted the remainder of us and then they selected all the young boys, including my brother and myself.

We were taken away from this barrack and were herded into another barrack. There must have been at least 800 of us. These barracks were originally made to keep horses in and were assembled by the prisoners themselves.

In the middle of the barrack was a low chimney and at the end of the building were latrines. We stayed in these barracks a few days.

Every morning and every evening we had to stand outside for the Appel (roll call). They counted us to make sure that nobody had escaped. One morning as we were standing outside, for the Appel, a group of SS men arrived and walked along the lines as we stood to attention.

They looked everybody up and down and then they picked out the healthy boys. My brother, who was younger than me, looked healthier than me; and he was told to join the other line. So I was left on my own with the rest of the boys. I didn't want to be apart from him, after we had been through so much together, so I took a chance and ran across to join him while the SS were not looking.

My brother and I were among the 131 boys selected from the 800 and we were moved into another barrack. The rest of the boys were all killed.

We had to undress then the SS gave us a medical examination. They asked us whether we had ever been ill or had any contagious diseases.

We were divided into three groups but to my dismay my brother Yitzchok was put in another group to me. There were also two brothers in the same position as us – they were also separated. So when the SS were busy we swapped places so that we could each be together with our brothers.

After this, some Jewish prisoners started tattooing numbers on our arms. Each one of us received a number on the left arm. My number is B 7660, and my brother's number is B 7661.

A few days later the SS accompanied by their large Alsatian dogs (they never went anywhere without the dogs) marched us out until we came to a place which was the main camp of Auschwitz.

Over the entrance was a sign which read 'Arbeit Macht Frei' (Work Makes you Free). As we came near the camp there was an air raid and we were ordered to lay down on the ground as the anti-aircraft guns went into action.

When the air raid was over the Guards marched us up to the gates of the camp. The leader of the guards went into the office and enquired where he should take us. We heard the Kommandant laugh and say "Straight to the crematorium."

The leader came out and said we should march with him. We were faint with hunger and terror but we didn't dare fall behind. We marched for about fifteen minutes then the leader ordered us to halt. We noticed soldiers with machine guns aimed at us. They were standing around laughing.

We were relieved when we were ordered to continue marching. Then we were led into solidly built blocks. When we came inside we couldn't believe our eyes. There were showers with mirrors and each one of us was allotted a bunk with a mattress.

We were given a bowl of soup together with a piece of bread and a piece of sausage. This was the first food we had eaten for three days.

A few hours later a doctor arrived and examined us again. We were told that we were to be quarantined in this block for three weeks, then we would be sent out to work. Later we learned that this camp was used as a model for the Red Cross Commission when they made their periodic inspections.

While we were in the main camp in Auschwitz we heard how Biebov had tricked Rumkovski. Apparently when his brother Joseph with his family were going to be deported, Biebov offered to take Rumkovski in his car to say goodbye to them. When Rumkovski and his family were in the carriage Biebov shook hands with them and took his leave.

Within seconds of his departure he turned round with a smile on his face and ordered the Germans to push another 80 people in the same carriage, then they bolted the door of the carriage. This was how Rumkovski and his family finally went to their death.

One day while we were in this camp our group of 26 boys were ordered to move some furniture to another part of the camp where there were a lot of Jewish girls. While we worked the girls gave us cups of coffee to drink which was sweetened with real sugar. We had not drunk real coffee with sugar for years.

When we looked around we realised we were in a brothel. The Germans had selected the most beautiful girls and had made them work as prostitutes for the SS.

When the three weeks were up armed German SS guards with their Alsatian dogs came and ordered us to get out. Then we marched for a few hours until we came to a place called Buddy, which was surrounded by a barbed wire electrified fence, overlooked by high watch towers.

The camp Kommandant came out and inspected us. He held a black leather whip under his arm. He picked out one boy – for no reason at all – and started whipping him. The boy was full of blood and couldn't stand. He had to be led away supported by other prisoners. This was done to frighten us.

His first words to us were: "In this place if you want to stay alive you will have to work very hard. You will have to get up every morning at 4 o'clock."

Buddy was a farm that supplied foodstuffs to the main camp of Auschwitz. Our group of boys was ordered to work in the stables. Some of the horses were riding horses used by the Gestapo, and the others were working horses.

It was our job to look after these horses, to feed them and to keep them clean. When we got up in the morning we had to prepare their food and give them water. We envied the care they received but most of all we envied them for their food.

In the evening when the horses came back we also had to feed them and to clean them from the dirt that had accumulated during the day. They were better looked after than we were.

Their fur had to shine as if it were polished. It was very hard work and very long hours. Horses are very clean animals and won't drink dirty water or lay down in mud like cows or pigs.

Food was only given to us once a day when we came home from work late at night. We were then given a bowl of watery soup with a thin slice of black bread.

A few weeks later we were delighted to learn we would be given a bowl of potatoes like the adults who also worked in the stables; because looking after the horses was considered hard work.

So in the evening we boys queued up with the grown ups to get our bowl of potatoes. But when it came to our turn the cook refused to give us any. He said that boys don't work as hard as men, so we were not entitled to any. When the SS officer heard this he was very annoyed and ordered the cook, who was a farmer, to give us our ration at once.

I worked with the horses for about two months. Then as winter approached I was transferred to look after the sheep, who were brought into sheds because of the cold. It was much easier to look after the sheep. We kept warm because most of the time we were indoors.

The sheep were fed with a mixture of potatoes and some cereal. We also had to give them straw and hay to eat. We boys managed to steal some of the potatoes from the sheep and ate them whenever we had an opportunity. We risked our lives doing this – but we were desperate for food. It was the only way we could survive.

There were also three specially trained sheepdogs to keep the sheep together when they were taken out in the fields. The Gestapo supplied meat for us to give to these sheepdogs.

I remember one day when it was bitterly cold outside and we were sitting in the barracks. As we were cooking the meat for the sheepdogs we took some of it to eat for ourselves.

Suddenly the door opened and in marched the Oberscharf-fuehrer who was in charge of the whole camp. He took in the situation at a glance. He knew that we were eating but he didn't say anything.

He asked us questions about the work we were doing, then he went out and rode away on his horse. We couldn't believe what a lucky escape we had had.

Some days we were taken to ponds where the Germans bred fish. We had to go into the ice-cold water and catch the fish for the Gestapo to eat. Sometimes we managed to hide a fish in our trousers. We tied the bottom of our trousers with string so that the fish couldn't slither out. It was a peculiar sensation to have live fish moving around in your trousers. Sometimes the fish had teeth.

When we got back to the barracks the Guards made us strip. If they found we were hiding any fish, not only did they confiscate it, but they gave us a good beating into the bargain.

But if we were successful in bringing it back with us, we either ate the fish ourselves, or exchanged it for bread with the other prisoners.

The air raids were getting more and more frequent both by day and by night. We prayed that we would soon be liberated from this living hell.

I shall never forget one of the most sadistic punishments we received. There were 26 of us boys in these barracks. We all came from Lodz. Every morning when the siren sounded we had to get up immediately, dress and make our bunk bed.

A few minutes later another siren sounded and we all had to be outside for the Appel. (These took place every morning and again in the evening when we came back from work).

In our barracks there was a boy called Faivel Dzialowski, who found out that in the next bock to ours there was a Hungarian Rabbi who had managed to smuggle into the camp a pair of Tefillin.

Every morning after he dressed he ran over to put on the Tefillin and we took it in turns to make his bunk so that he could be outside in time for the Appel together with us. There were three bunks, one on top of the other.

Once the boy whose turn it was to make Feivel's bed overslept and didn't have time to make it. That evening when we returned from work the SS Blockfuehrer called out: "Stube 18. Austreten!" So we stepped forward from the other prisoners. Then he told us to follow him into the barrack.

He pointed to the unmade bunk and asked "Who sleeps here?" Feivel Dzialowski put his hand up and the Blockfuehrer ordered all of us outside. Trembling with fear we followed.

Once outside the Blockfuehrer started whipping him and the SS guards beat him with their rifle butts. He was covered with blood and fell to the floor in agony. He had to be carried away and to this day he doesn't walk straight.

As a punishment we all had to stand for three hours in the freezing cold on top toes, with our arms held high. It was impossible to stand on our toes for longer than a few minutes at a time, and every time one of us put his heel down we were whipped unmercifully.

One morning at the end of November 1944, after the Appel, we were told not to go to work but to return to the barrack. Later that day there was loud gunfire from heavy artillery coming from the direction of the railway line which was nearby. Polish partisans had blown up a train carrying arms to the front line. This news gave us hope.

There was another incident that cheered us up. In our camp there was a Polish Kapo and a Jewish Kapo. (A Kapo was a prisoner in charge of other prisoners). They were hated by everybody. They both needed a dentist.

If we would have needed to see a dentist, nobody would have taken any notice but a Kapo had special privileges. There was no dentist in Buddy which was part of Birkenau so they had to travel to the main camp of Auschwitz.

The only way to get to Auschwitz was to travel on the wagon which brought food supplies to our camp every day. So these Kapos travelled on the food wagon, accompanied by two armed guards, to see the dentist.

We heard this story later. On the way to the main camp a car drove up and stopped the wagon. Two high ranking officers got out of the car and ordered the two Kapos to accompany them.

They produced documents that said these two Kapos were wanted in the main camp for questioning. They took the men away with them. When the SS guards arrived at the main camp and told their story it turned out that the two "high ranking officers" were actually Partisans.

There was a buzz of excitement when the news filtered through to us. It gave us hope that we were not forgotten by the outside world. Some day later the Blockfuehrer told us that these two men had been caught and executed. Whether it was true or not we shall never know.

About a month before the end of my stay in Auschwitz I managed to get a job with a Jewish tailor who worked outside the perimeter of the camp. He had a little workshop on the top floor of the barracks where the SS had their living quarters.

The tailor collected me every morning. He was accompanied by a SS guard. I was useful to the tailor because I had worked in the tailoring department in the Ghetto. So I was experienced in using the sewing machine and I could also sew by hand.

This tailor used to make uniforms for the officers. Every time one of them came up for fittings I wanted to hide in a corner as I was terrified they would do something to me.

More than once they would beat him up if they weren't satisfied with his work, or if the garment wasn't ready on time. Once an SS officer asked me to do some sewing for him. I didn't know exactly what he wanted so he took out his leather whip and thrashed me. Then he sneered "Do you know now what I want?"

While we were working in Birkenau, lorry loads of red ashes were brought in every day. We had to dig deep ditches to bury these ashes. In the ashes we found charred pieces of bones, then we realised that these ashes were from the Jews that were burned to death in the crematoriums.

They also brought in wagon loads of leather boots which were distributed to us; as it was impossible to work in the ditches without wearing high boots. We knew that these boots had been taken from the Jews that had been murdered.

Every week while we were standing in the Appel, detachments of SS officers would inspect us and select those boys and men who looked weak, and take them away. We never saw them again. Then they would bring others to take their place.

Some of the prisoners couldn't take the harsh regime and the cruelty. They committed suicide by touching the electric fence and were instantly electrocuted. It was nothing unusual to wake up in the morning to find dead bodies lying around.

There were a lot of factories around Auschwitz where the prisoners worked and they came under heavy bombardment mainly during the night. As we tried to sleep, the barracks used to vibrate from the noise of the bombs that were falling.

One day we heard that one of the crematoriums had been bombed and that some of the prisoners who worked there had managed to escape. They were called the Sonderkommado or

Kanada. The SS only kept these people alive for a few weeks and then they were killed and were replaced with other Jews.

At the end of December 1944 the Germans ordered us to dismantle all the farming machinery. We were sure that we were going to be killed as the crematoriums were still in full production. The sound of heavy gunfire continued, so we knew that the front line was getting nearer.

1945

One morning in January 1945 when we stood outside for the Appel we were told the camp was being evacuated and we would not be sent out to work anymore. We were not allowed to go back into the barrack but had to stand outside all day.

When it became dark we were ordered to start marching. We were surrounded by SS guards together with their vicious Alsatian dogs. They showed us no pity. It was bitterly cold. The snow was thick on the ground.

It was a silent shuffle of death to a destination that offered nothing but hopelessness. We were helpless. We were not soldiers in a war but innocent boys. Whoever couldn't keep up with the others was shot on the spot. The roads were littered with dead bodies. Nobody wanted to be left behind. It was a pitiful sight to see boys crawling on their hands and knees trying to keep up with the others.

The high-ranking SS officers travelled by car, on lorries or rode on horses. The guards had to march with us. We marched for three days and three nights.

The Russians were on our tail which made us very happy, but the SS guards were afraid that they would be taken prisoner. The Russian aeroplanes flew very low. They could see us by the flare of the bombs they dropped which lit up the area.

On the third night we were marched into a school during an air raid and we laid down on the floor. When the air raid was over we couldn't get up, as it was the first rest we had had for 72 hours.

In the middle of the night an SS officer entered the school and ordered us to stand on our feet. The guards who had accompanied us remonstrated with him saying they were exhausted.

He walked over to them and took out a revolver. He asked: "Who is too tired to stand up?" The guards got frightened and quickly stood up. At the same time they pushed us out and beat us with their rifle butts as they did so.

I was faint from hunger and collapsed as we were marching. My brother Yitzchok revived me with some snow so that I could carry on walking.

We walked for another few kilometres until it got light, then we arrived at a railway station where an empty coal train was waiting. The wagons were full of snow which we had to clear with our bare hands before we could get on.

When the train started moving we were all exhausted and we could hardly stand. We travelled for two days without food or water. We kept alive by eating snow. Then the train stopped outside a camp called Grosrosen.

We waited there for about 6 hours. The SS guards were told there was no room in the camp for us, so the train started off again. We heard later that we were lucky not to have gone into this camp as nobody survived. The inmates had all been killed off.

We travelled all night. In the morning we were surrounded by dead bodies. We were ordered to throw them out into the snow. Then the Germans picked out some men from the train to dig ditches and to bury the corpses.

We travelled like this from Auschwitz until we arrived at Buchenwald concentration camp. The journey lasted seven weary days and every morning we had to repeat the ordeal of throwing off the frozen dead bodies and burying them in ditches, wherever the train stopped.

All this time we were not given any food to eat or water to drink. The only clothing we had was the thin striped uniform that had been issued to us in Auschwitz. As we travelled in open wagons and the snow was falling continuously this was frozen to our bodies.

From a transport of 5,000 people that left Auschwitz only a few hundred survived; these were mainly youngsters. The adults did not have the resistance to withstand the terrible conditions.

We were glad to reach Buchenwald after the horrendous train journey. There we were deloused, our bodies shaved of all hair, and we had a shower. They gave us fresh striped uniforms as the ones we were wearing were in tatters.

The Germans then made us queue up and camp officials took down our particulars. We had to tell them where we came from and the number tattooed on our arms. They didn't ask us for our names – they didn't consider them important.

Finally we were given a small bowl of soup and a piece of black bread and were led into barrack No. 66.

Every morning and every evening we had to stand in lines of five for the Appel. All the beatings and hanging took place at these Appels and we had to stand and watch as these atrocities were carried out. We used to stand for hours on end.

Many of our boys dropped dead from exhaustion, from the cold and from hunger. When we looked out from the barracks there were dead bodies all over the place. These were then piled up and put on hand carts to be taken to the crematoriums. It is difficult to describe the gruesome scenes that we watched every day.

While we were in Buchenwald we had to get up at half past three in the morning and be outside for the Appel by four o'clock. Then we used to travel into the city of Weimar by train, which was about ten kilometres away.

We were assigned to work in the bombed houses. The Germans were frightened to go in as it was dangerous because of the falling masonry, but we were expendable. We had to bring out all the dead bodies and anything else we could see.

While we were working in the houses if we found any food we used to hide it in our trousers. We tied the trouser bottoms with string so that the food wouldn't fall out.

Very often when we returned to Buchenwald the guards would notice that we were hiding something and they would make us strip. Then they confiscated the few miserable scraps of food that we had smuggled in and gave us a good beating. But it didn't stop us from trying to smuggle in food as the few times we were successful made it all worthwhile.

All we had to eat when we returned to Buchenwald in the evening was a bowl of watery soup and a thin slice of black bread. If we were lucky there was a small piece of potato floating around in the soup. So whatever food we managed to scrounge we appreciated.

The air raids were getting more and more frequent and lasted longer and longer. In the beginning they took place only at night, but gradually they bombed during the day as well.

Around the site of Buchenwald there were a number of factories which were targeted for these bombing raids.

Meanwhile the noise of the gunfire was getting closer. There was some clandestine radios in the camp, and we heard that the Americans were not far away. They had already entered the town of Erfurt, which was near Buchenwald. We also heard rumours that the camp was soon going to be liquidated.

Buchenwald was a different type of camp from Auschwitz. In Buchenwald there were many different kinds of prisoners. Some of them were political ones brought in from all over Europe. One of these was Leon Blum, the Jewish Prime Minister of pre-war France. Others were army personnel who had previously escaped and had been sent to Buchenwald as a punishment.

These prisoners intended to organise themselves into a Resistance Movement and make an uprising against the Germans. They came into our barracks with long knives which they sharpened on stones. They also made crude weapons which they planned to use on the Germans.

However their plans came to nothing because all the small camps around Buchenwald were liquidated and the prisoners were sent in to our camp together with the guards who were well armed. They realised that if they made an uprising they would all be slaughtered.

In the meantime the SS stopped all supplies of food into the camp. They announced that a loaf of bread would be given out to everyone who voluntarily came to the gates of the camp. This was always their ploy to make us come out of hiding.

My brother Yitzchok and I made up our minds that we would not leave the barracks voluntarily. We hid ourselves in the loft of the barracks, together with some of the other boys, so that we wouldn't get taken away. To get to the loft we had to pull away some of the wooden boards of the ceiling and clamber up.

Suddenly the floor of the loft collapsed from the weight of

everyone and we all fell down. We had nowhere to hide when the SS came in and started to shoot. They killed a few boys and then ordered us to get out immediately, otherwise we would be shot as well. So we had no choice but to go.

We were pushed to the gates of the camp with rifle butts. There each one of us was given a small loaf of bread. This happened in the beginning of April 1945.

We were made to march for a few hours until we reached an empty coal wagon train. We were put on this train and waited about four hours until it started to move.

Then there was an air raid the planes came down very low. We could see that they were American planes. The pilots could see us. They knew that there was a concentration camp nearby in Buchenwald.

We travelled on the train until we came to a railway junction where the line was bombed, and we couldn't travel any further. It was chaos.

On the line next to ours there was a train standing with anti-aircraft guns ready to attack the planes. It was full of German soldiers and civilians trying to get away from the advancing American army.

Our train stopped at this junction for two days and then we started moving again. When we'd travelled a few miles the line was bombed again.

We 'stopped-started' like this for the next two weeks. All this time we were not given any food or water. If anyone tried to jump down from the wagon into the field to eat some grass, or maybe a cabbage, he was shot on the spot.

Whenever we stopped at a village the inhabitants were very kind and tried to give us some food, but each time they were driven away by the SS.

There were rumours that we were going to be given some soup in the evening. We couldn't wait for nightfall but when we started eating the soup it had a funny taste. It was also very salty but we were ravenous as we had had nothing to eat for two weeks so we wolfed it down.

In the morning we woke up to find loads of dead bodies all over the place. My stomach felt sore and my body was swollen; and so were the bodies of all the boys who were still alive.

We realised the Germans had poisoned the soup, which was why so many people had died after eating it. We tried to get water to quench our thirst but it was impossible as the SS shot anyone who got down from the train.

The nightmare journey seemed never-ending. When the train travelled in one direction, more than once the lines were down, and we had to go back and find another route.

After another week of slowly moving backwards and forwards we finally came to a halt. Then a group of German SS officers arrived and interrogated us. As it was spring time the farmers were looking for youngsters to help out on the farm.

They asked us our nationality and we told them we were Polish, but we didn't admit that we were Jews. They made us get down from the wagons and examined us.

They looked behind our ears, and on our necks, and studied the shape of our heads. They couldn't decide whether or not we were Jews so they ordered us to undress and looked to see who was circumcised.

The Head of the Commission said: "Sie sind alle Juden" (They are all Jews). Then we were told to get back on the wagons and the train started moving away.

It moved very slowly for a few hours then it stopped under a bridge because there was an air raid. The sky was full of Allied aeroplanes and bombs were falling all around us. The train deliberately stopped under a bridge because the Germans knew that the pilots would see that we were from the Concentration camps and so they hoped that the bridge would not be bombed.

The SS guards jumped off the train and crawled under the wagons to protect themselves from the bombs.

On the adjoining line we found out that there was a wagon full of food supplies. While the bombing was going on we forced open the wagon and we all grabbed whatever food we could lay our hands on.

I managed to seize a big basket of eggs, but the SS saw us

and started shooting. I managed to get back on to our wagon with the basket of eggs. Although most of them were broken, everyone descended on me, and within two minutes we had finished the eggs.

The next day some other SS officers arrived and they started to select the people who didn't have numbers tattooed on their arms. I was frightened that they could tell by the numbers that we were Jews, so I got hold of a piece of iron, heated it up, and attempted to burn off my number. I managed to burn off one number but it was too painful to continue, so I gave up. I have the scar to this day.

The people who had no numbers were led away. We were told to get back on to the wagons and the train moved away. We passed through town that had been completely raised to the ground by the bombs. Finally we arrived in Czechoslovakia.

The journey from the time we left Buchenwald until we reached Czechoslovakia took four weeks. We passed through famous spa towns like Marienbad and Carlsbad. They had all been destroyed by heavy bombing.

As soon as we crossed over the Czech border the Czechs tried to throw us food. They risked their lives to do this as the Germans guards kept shooting into the crowd, but this didn't stop them from trying.

The train stopped outside the Ghetto at Theresienstadt. Some Czech civilians mounted the train and asked the SS guards if they would like to have a bath and something to eat. They eagerly agreed and went off with them. We never saw the guards again and we realised that the men were Czech partisans.

We were taken into the Theresienstadt ghetto and were led into a 'Badeanstalt' (Bath house) and told to take a shower. Suddenly we heard a terrible bang and all the lights went out. We could hear the sound of heavy artillery and exploding bombs.

We laid down on the floor and tried to sleep, but it was impossible. The noise continued all night until daybreak, then suddenly there was silence. Cautiously we lifted up our heads and looked out of the window. There were soldiers running backwards and forwards with machine guns, ready to shoot. We couldn't see clearly what nationality they were.

Then one of the boys shouted out: "The Russians are here! The Russians are here!" We all rushed out into the street and we jumped on the Russian tanks which were advancing towards us. They welcomed us and we all drove together to a town called Leitmaritz which was nearby.

Then it dawned on us that we were free. Free from the German sadists, free from the German atrocities and free from starvation. We couldn't believe it. It took some days for us to realise that we had managed to survive this living hell, while so many of our companions had perished in unspeakable agony.

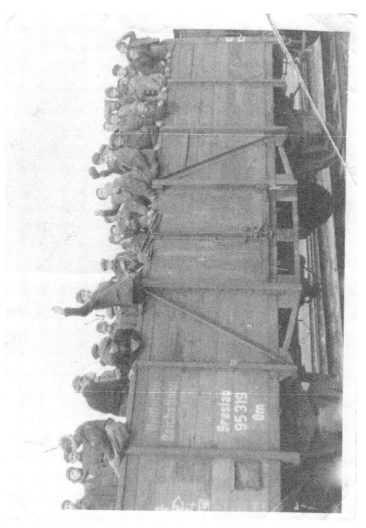

Myself (left) and Yitzchok (middle) about to be liberated in Theresienstadt

Liberation

We raided the German shops of all the goods that were there. I remember picking up a jar of blackberries and putting them in a big box. It was very heavy and I could hardly carry it. Then I saw a young German girl on a bicycle and I commandeered it. I put the heavy box on the back of the bicycle and rode it back to the camp.

Lots of the boys brought back loaves of bread under their arms and in sacks. After a few days the bread became mouldy and we had to throw it away. Adults had more sense and took more valuable things like jewellery. We could only think of food!

We were allotted some rooms from the Ghetto Verwaltung where we could stay. They were completely empty of furniture. There were not even any beds so we had to sleep on the bare boards on the floor but after what we had gone through it was paradise.

The Red Cross started to send in parcels of food and we fell on them with delight. But after so long a time of near starvation and malnutrition our digestions couldn't take the rich food.

The next day two boys went down with a high fever and the next day some more. A Russian army doctor was hurriedly called in and he diagnosed typhoid. One by one we all came down with it.

I was delirious most of the time. I suffered blinding headaches and I had a very high temperature. There were no medicines available, only Russian vodka. The fever lasted three weeks and it drained all the energy out of me.

I became very weak and it was impossible for me to get out of bed until the fever subsided. My brother Yitzchok also had the same symptoms.

There were no hospitals and no beds. They took wardrobes from the Ghetto apartments, laid them on the floor and scattered straw over them for us to lay on. We were covered with thin grey army blankets.

Many boys died from the typhoid. It was ironic that they had endured such horrific experiences and managed to survive the war; and now after the liberation they died from the epidemic.

While we were in the hospital we heard that each government had sent trains to take their nationals back to their country of origin. When we realised that the Polish government had also sent such a train we quickly discharged ourselves from the hospital.

I never wanted to return to Poland. To me, Lodz had become a graveyard, and I could not face the prospect of resuming life there. Most of the atrocities that had taken place were on Polish

139

soil.

In order that we should not be picked up by the Polish officials we hid ourselves until the train with the Polish repatriates had gone. Most of the people who were picked up by the Poles were stretcher cases, as they were not able to escape.

We scrounged food when and where we could. Luckily for us there was an organised food distribution system in operation, so we managed to get by. In any case, we had had experience of slow starvation in the camps, so it was no hardship to us.

Eventually when we recovered our strength we boys formed into a group. We were given permission from the Russian Commandant to bring in German prisoners of war from a nearby camp, to clean up the houses and to sweep the streets in the Ghetto.

It was amazing how quickly we took over the role of oppressor. However weak and undernourished we were, we looked like living skeletons, nevertheless they were terrified of us.

The Germans had been good teachers for us, but we could not bring ourselves to do them any bodily harm. But we did humiliate them, making them scrub the streets again and again.

Not every German prisoner that we brought into work was an SS man. The majority of Germans belonged to the Wehrmacht (the German army), only the elite belonged to the SS.

One day we found a ring worn by one of the prisoners which

had the skull and crossbones engraved on it. It was the same emblem on the caps worn by the members of the SS. When we asked one of the men if it belonged to him he denied it, but we knew he wasn't telling the truth as we saw the SS tattoo under his armpit, so finally he had to admit it.

Every morning we brought in a group of German prisoners to work. Before they returned to the camp they had to be counted. One day there were two missing, so we had to go into the houses to search for them.

When we finally found them we learned that they had been hidden and fed by a German woman who had been married to a Jew, and that was why she was in the Ghetto. She said that she had "felt sorry for them."

In the meantime we heard rumours that we would be going to Palestine. We all wanted to go to Palestine but the British government didn't allow us in. Then we heard that we might be going to Switzerland to recuperate in the mountains, but these rumours came to nothing.

One day in July 1945 we were told to pack our belongings (not that we had much to pack) and we were put on a train to Prague. When we arrived there we stayed in a building which had been the Headquarters of the Gestapo. The outside of the building was full of bullet holes.

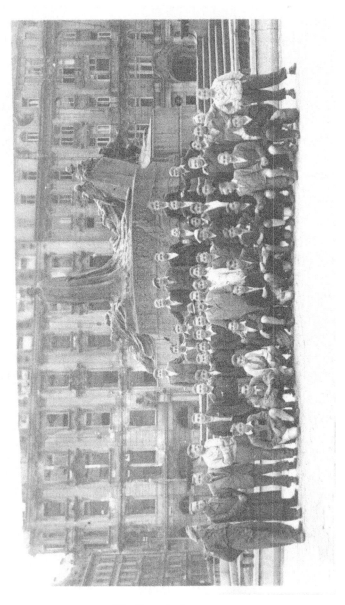

The Boys in Prague

We stayed in Prague for a few days while we waited for the planes that would take us to England. We were treated very kindly by the Czechs. They knew that we were ex-camp inmates because our heads had been shaved and our hair had not yet had much chance to grow.

Also our clothes were a mish-mash. A hat from here, shorts from somewhere else, a jacket that was three sizes too big. When we went anywhere by bus they didn't want to take the fare from us. Even in the restaurants and cinemas they didn't charge us.

A few days later we were taken by bus to an airport and then we were air lifted to England in RAF bomber planes, which still had machine guns mounted at the back of the planes. There were no seats in the plane and we had to sit on the floor. The pilot told us not to touch anything.

We were flown to an airport called Carlisle, and from there we were taken by coach to Windermere which is in the Lake District in the North of England; to start a new life in a strange country with a strange language. I was 18 when I arrived in Windermere; a teenager in years but an old man in experience.

We were driven to a compound which during the war had been used to house workers of a nearby aircraft factory. Each one of us was allotted a very small room which was furnished with a bed, a built-in wardrobe and a table and chair. To us it was the height of luxury. There were communal showers and a large dining hall where we ate all our meals.

In the mornings we were given cooked porridge with bread and butter and lots of milk. The bread disappeared as soon as it was put on the table. We were not used to eating white bread. To us it was like cake.

Also, because we were frightened the supplies would run out, we used to hide it under the table and then take it back to our rooms.

The helpers in the kitchen couldn't understand how we could get through so much bread. After a few days we saw that the bread was getting stale and mouldy and had to be thrown away. So we stopped hiding the bread as we realised that it wasn't necessary any longer.

We started putting on weight as we ate so much bread and porridge. I didn't really like the porridge, but I ate it, lumps and all, because they told us it was healthy.

Many Jewish organisations, religious and non-religious, had sent in madrichim (leaders) to be in charge of us. Each organisation tried to get as many boys as they could.

There was a Rabbi there called Rabbi Theodor Weiss who was one of the madrichim. He had a warm personality and he was very popular with us boys. He brought us back to normality.

He gave us lessons every day and taught us among other things about religion, how to behave and how to play football. During the summer we had English lessons. He was with us the whole time we were in Windermere, until we arrived in London.

I will always be grateful to him. He later became Chief Rabbi in Zurich, Switzerland.

Then in the autumn it was decided to close down the camp and we were told we would be sent to various hostels throughout England.

I wanted to go to a Yeshiva to learn about Judaism, so I decided to go to a hostel in London that was under the auspices of the Etz Chaim Yeshiva in Thrawl Street, E.L.

Together with 14 other boys we were sent to a hostel in Woodberry Down, North London. We each received 10 shillings pocket money, from which we had to pay all personal expenses, including toiletries, toothpaste, fares etc.

I went to the yeshivah for two years and at the same time studied English at St. Martin's college of Art in Charing Cross Road. Although I was encouraged by the late Rabbi Eliyahu Lopian (who was Rosh Yeshivah at the time) to stay on in the Yeshivah, when the two years was up I decided that it was time to think of making a living.

I really wanted to do cutting and designing, so I contacted Mr. Montefiore who was in charge of the committee that brought us over. He told me that he would pay for me to attend a course at the Tailor & Cutter Academy to learn the trade.

At the Academy they told me it was pointless only learning theory, so in order to get practical experience I took on a job with a tailor in the West End as an apprentice.

When my course at the Tailor & Cutter Academy finished I started studying at the Regent Street Polytechnic. I attended classes two or three times a week for three years.

When they closed the hostel I found lodgings with a family called Schmahl, who originally came from Vienna. They were very good to me and treated me like a son.

At that time everyone was anxious to find any relatives who were still alive. Although from 200,000 Jews who had populated the Lodz Ghetto only a few thousand survived. We were still hoping against hope that our sister and our mother were still alive.

However, it appeared that from a close family of 300 people which included uncles, aunts, male cousins and female cousins, only seven of us had survived.

Myself after the war

My tailor shop in Stamford Hill

Then I remembered that before the war my parents had often spoken of cousins who lived in Toronto, Canada, called Warga. So I wrote them a letter. I didn't know the exact address but the Post Office made an effort and traced them.

A few weeks later I received a letter from one of my cousins in Canada, inviting my brother and myself to come over to Toronto. They also sent us a parcel of clothing.

I went to Canada on my own, as in the meantime my brother had emigrated to what was then Palestine. In Toronto I worked in a tailoring factory. I stayed there for two years but I missed my friends and came back to England for a holiday.

I was happy when I dated a young attractive girl called Freda soon after I returned to London and I was overjoyed a few months later when she accepted my proposal of marriage.

We were married on the 24th May 1953 in Dean Street Synagogue in London W.L. The chupa was given by the late Rabbi Sperber and the reception and dinner was held at Folman's, which at the time was a very famous Kosher restaurant.

Our wedding took place a week before the coronation of Queen Elizabeth. I remember that the streets were decorated with flags and flowers in honour of the occasion, but in my heart, I believed they were for Freda and myself. It is truly a miracle that a human being can rise above constant deprivation and degradation and still make a new and meaningful life.

Freda and I on our wedding day

Thank G-d, Freda and I now have three children. The oldest one is called Lea, who is named after my mother, Pinchas (usually called Pinny) who is named after my father, and Helen who is named after Freda's mother. They are all married and we have twelve grandchildren.

My brother Yitzchok now lives in Israel with his wife Dalia, and three children. His two oldest children are named after my parents and youngest boy is called Jacob. He has seven grandchildren. I know that G-d didn't forget us!

Postscript

I'm often asked by young people today, and especially young Israelis, how could this genocide have happened in a country like Poland where there were 3.5 million Jews.

At the outbreak of the Second World War big cities like Warsaw had half a million Jews and Lodz had a quarter of a million Jews. So how could it have happened that so many Jews let themselves be led to the slaughter by the Germans?

It's very hard to imagine today what the conditions were like then. You have to understand first of all that the Jews in Poland were living in the middle of a hostile community.

The Poles were the first ones to collaborate with the Germans against the Jews. Although they hated the Germans, they hated the Jews even more, so they were more than ready to co-operate with killing off the Jews.

Also, the Germans did not start straight away with mass killings. When they first entered Poland they took away our legal rights, then commandeered the business. (Jews were not allowed to own any business).

Their next move was to take away all the professional people (doctors, teachers, communal leaders). Then they took away the able-bodied men. This left families frightened and defenceless.

Then they made the Jews give up all their valuables (money, jewels etc.), and forced them to leave their living quarters and move into the Ghetto.

Once we were herded into the Ghetto we were doomed, although we didn't realise it at the time. With no possessions, no money, no food and no able-bodied men around to protect us, we had no resistance.

Families were cruelly broken up. Parents were forced to give away their little children to certain death. So they had no reason to go on living.

Also, as a result of overcrowding, starvation and lack of heating and sanitation, thousands died from infectious diseases. The Nazis were intent upon creating such conditions that made it impossible for any normal human being to survive.

You have to bear in mind that some of the German SS were a well organised gang of thugs, who, with the approval of the authorities, terrorised us both physically and mentally.

Others were intellectuals who were obsessed with the Nazi ideology of wiping out the Jewish race, which they considered vermin.

Although these were educated men with families, nevertheless they carried out the most cruel and cold-blooded atrocities to the Jews.

After my mother and my sister were sent to the gas chamber in Auschwitz, there was just my brother and myself left. We helped each other as best we could.

If we would have been left completely on our own, I don't think either of us would have been able to survive.

Myself and Yitzchok

Alexander Riseman passed away on 21st March 2016/11th Adar Sheini 5776

Alexander didn't speak for several years about his experience and this book was only written when his wife, Freda, forced him to document his experiences. He then started to see that Holocaust denial was becoming fashionable and decided to speak up. He gave numerous talks about his experiences, as well as writing this book to ensure his life and his family's legacy would never be denied or forgotten.

ק"ק הנדון עדת ישראל
HENDON ADATH YISROEL CONGREGATION
11 BRENT STREET N.W.4

Cordially invite all Ladies and Gentlemen to hear

MR SENDER RISEMAN נ"י
(Auschwitz survivor)

who will speak in the **Shul Hall**

about his experiences of the SHOAH

on

Sunday the 6ᵗʰ of August 2000 – אב מנחם ה

at 8pm

(מנחה–ומעריב at 7:30 PM)

Young people are especially welcome !

Speech at Hachnosos Sefer Torah - Toras Chaim Shul NW4 - Sunday 17th June 2007

D ayanim, Rabbonim, Gabboim, family and friends.

I would like to welcome you all here tonight to celebrate the Hachnosos Sefer Torah in memory of my dear parents and my sister 'zichronom levracha,' and my late dear wife Freda 'oleho hasholom.'

A special welcome to all my family that have come from Switzerland, and also to my machatainista Mrs Elzas from The Hague, Holland, and, last but not least, my son Rabbi Pinchos Riseman from Israel, who has written this Sefer Torah.

I wish to thank Josy and Jenny Orenstein and my daughter Helen for all the help they have given me with the organisation of this simcha.

In the 'chazoras hashatz' (the Chazzans repetition) of the Yom Kippur Mussaf service we recite the story of the 'asoroh harigei malchus' - the 10 martyrs that were killed by the Romans.

Before they were going to kill Rabbi Chanania ben Tradiyon the Romans took away the Sefer Torah that Rabbi Chanania always carried with him and wrapped it around him. Before they set him and the Sefer Torah on fire Rabbi Chanania said to this daughter and to this talmidim 'they can burn me and they can burn the parchment of the Sefer Torah but they cannot burn the letters in the Sefer Torah – they will stay alive and they will fly up in heaven.'

Every year when I recite this story, it reminds me of the time when the Germans entered my home town of Lodz in Poland in 1939. They rounded up the Gabboim of all the shuls in the city, and they made them hand over the keys of all their respective shuls.

A few weeks later they gave back the keys to the gaboim of the largest shul in Lodz. This shul had a capacity of 1500 seats – it was one of the most beautiful and impressive shuls in Europe. They ordered the gaboim to fill up the shul with Jews and all the men were made to wear their taleisim, while the chazzan and the choir were forced to recite the Yom Kippur service. All this was filmed by the Nazis, as they wanted to use this film as a preservation record of an extinct race they had once existed.

A few days later all the shuls in the city were burned down, including the Sifrei Torah and all the ornaments inside. Little did they know that they were able to burn down the shuls and Sifrei Torah, but they were not able to destroy the 'oisios' – the letters....the very same 'oisios' that were flying in the air at the time of Rabbi Chanania ben Tradiyon's death. Today we are all here to celebrate the completion of a new Sefer Torah containing all these letters - a new Sefer Torah that has been written by my son, Pinchas, the son of a Holocaust survivor. And, it is not just the oisios that we are celebrating here, we are also celebrating new generations of my family - my children, my grandchildren and my great-grandchildren who are B'H learning and living according to these oisios, and will hopefully carry on the derech, the way, of our ancestors.

Now I would like to say a few words about my dear parents, Pinchos and Lea Riseman, my sister Rachel, zichronom livrocho, and my dear late wife Freda oleyho hasholom.

When the war in Poland started in 1939 both my parents were in their 30's. My father was one of the first Jews to be killed by the Nazis in 1940 as we were being herded into the Lodz Ghetto and my mother and my sister were killed 4 years later in August 1944 when we were all deported to Auschwitz. Only my brother Yitschak and myself survived the war.

My parents were very good to us and had BH a happy marriage. They both worked very hard to give us a comfortable life. My mother had an open house and ear for people who needed help and advice - she was known as "Die Klige Lea" - my Freda Oleh hashalom was a lot like her. My father was killed a few months before my barmitzvah. He was a very caring and honest man and was very concerned about our Chinuch. He sent us to the most expensive school in Lodz and when we went on our annual long summer vacations in the forest he would hire a private Rebbe to come up to our cottage every day from Lodz to give my brother, my sister and I private Koidesh lessons. My older sister Rachel was a tremendous support to my widowed mother during

161

the terrible years in the Lodz ghetto and when my mother was selected to be gassed on arrival at Auschwitz Rachel opted to accompany her mother, even though she knew this would mean certain death.

Now I would like to say a few words about my dearly beloved late wife Freda oleyo hasholom. I was honoured and privileged to be married to Freda for 48 years. With her help and loving kindness I was zoicher to rebuild my life and together we were blessed with a lovely Jewish home which Freda always filled with laughter and a tremendous positive attitude to life. Here I would like to stress that it was Freda who had the main responsibility of bringing up our three children, Lea, Pinny and Helen. As a devoted Jewish mother she instilled in them the strong love of Yiddishkeit which they practice in their respective homes today.

Freda was a perfectionist – she put her whole neshomo into everything she did, whether it be a poem for a Choson and Kallo, an article, a speech or even a letter. She would sit for hours and go over the text just to make sure it was perfect and always made sure that she finished off with a joke.

Freda had a bubbly personality and enjoyed making people laugh. Thanks to Freda, number 2 Holmdale Gardens was a friendly and open house. She loved having guests and we enjoyed many a Shabbos and Yom Tov meal surrounded by guests of all ages and from all backgrounds. Through her boundless energy, her love of life and her interest for others she was very popular and we were fortunate in having very many good friends – friends who I would like to sincerely thank tonight for continuing this friendship by inviting me regularly on Shabbos, Yom Tov and to their family simchas. I really appreciate this.

Through her work and social activities she often came into contact with very important and well-known people and it was through these connections that we were invited to attend the Queens Garden Party in Buckingham Palace in July 1993. You can imagine how proud I was standing next to my Freda when she was introduced to the Queen and Prince Phillip.

As you can imagine, life with Freda was never boring. There was always some new scheme being planned, new courses, new evening classes. She made use of every spare minute of her time and yet she managed to combine her busy schedule with raising her family and helping others. She even had a list of numbers of people next to the telephone whom she would regularly call to enquire how they were getting on and always made time to visit people who were not well.

We pray to Hashem that in the zechus of all the things that Freda accomplished in her lifetime and in the zechus of the new Sefer Torah being presented here today, which is dedicated to the memory of my dear parents zichronom levrocho, and my sister and Freda aleyhem hasholom, that their neshomos should rest in Gan Eden and be a meilitz yosher for all of us here and Klal Yisroel.

People have asked me why I am presenting this Sefer Torah to this shul and not to the Hendon Adath where I normally daven.

Well, the first reason is that I wanted to give this Sefer to a kehilla where it would be used frequently and I know that the Hendon Adath already has many beautiful Sifrei Torah and would not really have used this one very much. The second reason is our connection to Family Orenstein who are very involved in the running of this Shul. Salek Orenstein and I met after the war, we came over to this country together and were good friends every since. Salek was like a brother to me and Jenny and my late wife Freda were very close friends, like sisters. Our families used to go on holiday together and our children have remained good friends. Even today, Salek's children and grandchildren call me Uncle Sender and include me in their family and they have been very good to me since Freda's petira. To conclude, I would like to wish this kehilla that should go mechoyil el choyil, and the new Sefer Torah should be used on many happy occasions.

*Myself at the Hachnosas Sefer Torah, written by my son Pinchos
(left)*